PENGUIN BOOKS

"STOP TREATING ME LIKE A KID!"

ROBIN GOLDSTEIN, M.A., is a specialist in child development and the author of *Everyday Parenting: The First Five Years* and *More Everyday Parenting: The Six-to Nine-Year-Old*. She is a parenting consultant who has worked with families for many years and an adjunct faculty member at Trinity College in Washington, D.C., specializing in child development. In addition, she writes a newspaper column on child rearing. Robin Goldstein and her husband and two children live in Maryland.

JANET GALLANT is a writer, editor, and adjunct professor of English at Montgomery College in Rockville, Maryland. She collaborated with Robin Goldstein on *Everyday Parenting* and *More Everyday Parenting*. She is also the author of a recent children's book. She lives with her husband and two sons in Rockville, Maryland.

**ALSO BY ROBIN GOLDSTEIN
WITH JANET GALLANT**

Everyday Parenting:
The First Five Years

More Everyday Parenting:
The Six- to Nine-Year-Old

"STOP TREATING ME LIKE A KID!"

EVERYDAY PARENTING:
the 10- to 13-Year-Old

ROBIN GOLDSTEIN with JANET GALLANT

PENGUIN BOOKS

PENGUIN BOOKS

Published by the Penguin Group
Penguin Books USA Inc., 375 Hudson Street,
New York, New York 10014, U.S.A.
Penguin Books Ltd, 27 Wrights Lane,
London W8 5TZ, England
Penguin Books Australia Ltd, Ringwood,
Victoria, Australia
Penguin Books Canada Ltd, 10 Alcorn Avenue,
Toronto, Ontario, Canada M4V 3B2
Penguin Books (N.Z.) Ltd, 182–190 Wairau Road,
Auckland 10, New Zealand

Penguin Books Ltd, Registered Offices:
Harmondsworth, Middlesex, England

First published in Penguin Books 1994

10   9   8   7   6   5   4   3   2   1

Copyright © Robin Goldstein, 1994
All rights reserved

Illustrated by Ari Goldstein, Anna Goldstein, and Michael Gallant

Library of Congress Cataloging in Publication Data
Goldstein, Robin.
Stop treating me like a kid: everyday parenting: the
10- to 13-year-old/ Robin Goldstein with Janet Gallant.
p.   cm.
ISBN 0 14 01.7945 3
1. Child rearing.   2. Parenting.   I. Gallant, Janet.   II. Title.
HQ769.G666   1994
649'.1—dc20   93–36032

Printed in the United States of America
Set in Sabon   Designed by Jessica Shatan

Except in the United States of America, this book is sold
subject to the condition that it shall not, by way of trade
or otherwise, be lent, re-sold, hired out, or otherwise
circulated without the publisher's prior consent in any form
of binding or cover other than that in which it is published
and without a similar condition including this condition
being imposed on the subsequent purchaser.

With love,
to my husband, Miles,
my children, Ari and Anna,
and my parents,
Cynthia and Harold Reznick

ACKNOWLEDGMENTS

I want to thank my children for their understanding and for the inspiration they never fail to give. My husband patiently offered help and guidance through all stages of my research and writing. I am especially grateful to Janet Gallant, whose friendship I treasure, for her continuous help, consideration, and warmth.

CONTENTS

CHANGES

"DO I LOOK OKAY?"

INDEPENDENCE

RESPONSIBILITY

PEERS

EVERYDAY CONFLICTS

BIGGER PROBLEMS

INTRODUCTION

"I wish my child weren't so moody."
"I want my kids to be more respectful."
"Am I too strict?"
"Should 10-year-olds go to the movies by
  themselves?"
"My son's so busy I hardly see him."
"Do all 12-year-olds act like this?"

Parents watch with mixed emotions as their child moves through the pre-teen and early adolescent years. There is joy in seeing a child blossom and become more independent. But there is also frustration and worry. Issues range from the mundane (too much time on the phone, arguments over hairstyles) to the complex (talking about sex and puberty, dealing with divorce) to the truly frightening (drug and alcohol use).

As everyday issues become more complex, parents sometimes feel they're losing control in the family. They wonder if they've been effective: "Maybe I should have been firmer." "I wish I were more patient." They often don't understand their child's actions and don't see clear-cut answers to difficult questions. And most of all, they wonder, "Is it too late to make a difference?"

Be assured that you *can* still make a difference. You are vitally important at this stage in your child's life; you are the person best able to guide your child's character and behavior in positive ways. The doubts you feel are shared by most parents of pre-teens, just as the behavior you often despair of is common to most 10- to 13-year-olds. *"Stop Treating Me Like a Kid!"* is written to reassure you, to let you know what your child is thinking and feeling, and to offer you practical, everyday advice.

Pre- and early adolescence is a time of transition and great changes. There is the rapid physical growth and sexual development experienced by many children these ages. In addition, children approaching puberty develop a heightened awareness of themselves and the world. Their thoughts are more organized. They reason more logically, and they think about the future and about hypothetical and abstract ideas.

As they develop a set of values and sense of morality, pre-teens and early adolescents often say what's on their minds. In a positive way, your child may share her feelings more openly with you. However, she may also complain and criticize. "Why won't you listen to me?" "You just don't understand!"

Children increasingly seek independence and acceptance as they approach 13. They want to spend more time with peers and less with family, they want privacy, and they want to make their own decisions. As a result, parents must constantly make difficult decisions as their children push the limits. "When do I let go? When should I hold on?"

As this book will show you, 10- to 13-year-olds need a lot of guidance, support, and supervision. To effectively steer your child away from impulsiveness and toward a responsible, confident adolescence, you have to know where he is, what he's doing, and with whom. And your child has to know what is and isn't acceptable and what the consequences of misbehavior are.

The best way to help your child is to strengthen your relationship with him. Throughout this book, you will be urged to talk more with your child, listen to him, consider his point of view, do things together, take an interest in his activities, supervise him, set limits, and encourage him to pursue his own interests and talents. It is these basic tasks of parenting—and not quick fixes—that determine the success of pre- and early adolescence.

"Stop Treating Me Like a Kid!" is designed to be a reference and source of help and reassurance for parents of 10- to 13-year-olds. Issues are arranged by major categories, with separate articles for specific concerns. Each article is self-contained, so you can begin reading anywhere. Many of the articles complement each other, so you'll gain a fuller understanding of a topic if you read all the articles in a particular section.

Throughout the book, both sexes are treated equally: Articles using the pronoun "he" alternate with ones using "she." In most cases, however, what is said about one sex can be applied to the other.

Use "*Stop Treating Me Like a Kid!*" as a guide to everyday problems and conflicts. It can give you insight and set you in the right direction. If you'd like a more comprehensive discussion of some of the issues presented here, check the suggested reading list at the end of the last article. The list can direct you to books specializing in some of the more complex topics raised here.

TALKING
AND LISTENING

My Child Won't
Listen to My Side

Parents usually have good reasons for offering advice and guidance. From an adult perspective, they can see behavior in context and understand consequences. They give advice in order to help their child.

Yet children often reject their parents' lessons. What seems like good advice to an adult may sound like nagging to a child. "You'd get a better grade if your paper were neater." "Homework before TV." "Try to get along with your sister." Many 10- to 13-year-olds react negatively to their parents' words, especially if they don't like the ideas or suggestions presented: "Leave me alone!" "Okay, okay, I hear you!"

What a child reacts to sometimes is the way advice is presented. Anything that sounds like a lecture is rejected: "I was your age once, and . . ." "You really should . . ." "You must stop . . ." "I know what's

3

best . . ." After hearing his child's karate instructor speak about discipline, one father tried adding his own thoughts on the subject. "Dad, I already heard all this," his son said.

Most often, children don't pay attention because they themselves feel unheard. In the rush to give advice, parents don't always listen to what their child has to say. Instead, they interrupt him, ignore his words, or dismiss his arguments. Once a child believes that his parents aren't listening, he stops being receptive when they speak. Instead, he shows anger and frustration. "You don't understand!" He rolls his eyes, looks exasperated, stomps off, or slams his door, shutting out whatever advice his parents offer.

This, of course, leaves parents feeling upset and confused. They want to get their opinions across, but they don't know how. Many parents become harsh and demanding because they fear losing control over their child. They listen less and become more rigid in an attempt to make a point. Everyone is unhappy, and good advice goes unheard.

Communication doesn't have to be this antagonistic —families can learn to speak and listen in friendlier, more respectful ways. A first step to improving communication is letting your child express his opinions, even when they differ from yours. If your child makes a seemingly unreasonable request, don't respond with an automatic "No!" Instead, let him explain his side. He will feel heard, even if you turn down his request, and the fact that you listened to his ideas will make it easier for him to pay attention to your ideas and advice.

Consider the words and tone you use when speaking to your child. One parent lost his temper when his son asked for $10. "What is it now? All I hear from you is 'I need money.' You've gotten enough!" Angry words like these, or put-downs, can make your child feel too defensive to listen to you. Instead, he'll focus on defending himself when he finally has a chance to speak. If you use a patient, friendlier tone ("I know you'd like $15 for a T-shirt, but your blue shirt is still practically new"), your child may not come around to your point of view, but at least he'll feel less threatened. He'll have an easier time listening to you and he'll have an example of respectful communication to imitate.

To increase give-and-take in family communication, try asking your child questions before offering your opinions. "What do you think you should do about your room?" "Why do you think Joey's parents let him stay outside so late?" When you disagree on an issue, ask, "Why do you think Dad and I don't want to say yes?" By this age, your child should be able to predict your reasoning.

Take your time when responding to your child's requests, especially ones that make you angry. A moment spent considering your answer will give you time to calm down and will give your child a chance to rethink what he's said. If you want to bring up a troublesome issue, try to choose a calm time and then take a few minutes to plan your advice or instructions. "We need to talk about how your short temper is affecting the rest of the family." Your child will listen more readily to your reasonable statements than to a sudden outburst.

On some important or immediate issues, you will want your child to listen to you without discussion. "It's not safe to play around that way." "You must change your tone of voice." As long as your child doesn't always feel backed into a corner, unable to have his opinions heard, he will listen and respond when your words are urgent.

You may worry that you'll lose parental control if you allow your child to express his thoughts. However, letting him speak won't interfere with your ability to set limits. Instead, it will create an atmosphere of mutual respect, making it easier for him to listen to you.

Throughout his life, your child will encounter people with different points of view and different ideas. The positive communication skills you model for him now will help him get along with his family and with others in the future. He'll grow up saying, "My parents didn't let me do everything I wanted, but at least they listened."

I Want My Child to Be More Respectful

Getting children to be respectful seems a never-ending struggle. Parents start working on this issue when their child is a preschooler. They continue through the early elementary years and are still giving reminders when their child is in middle school. Despite increasing maturity, most 10- to 13-year-olds have to be told how to treat siblings, parents, teachers, coaches, and peers. Children these ages do understand why they should treat people kindly. They can imagine themselves in another person's place, they know what it's like to be teased and have hurt feelings, and they think about the impact of their behavior. Yet, for a number of reasons, they can't consistently translate their understanding into respectful action.

Some children are disrespectful because of the way they've been treated at home. Children imitate their

7

parents, and if a child's thoughts, feelings, and ideas have been ridiculed, she will criticize and be inconsiderate of others. One mother told her child to stop being rude, then said, "Just shut up and leave me alone." Another parent constantly found fault: "Why are you so lazy and disorganized?" Children copy such words and attitudes.

Unfortunately, school is another place children learn disrespect. Most teachers have rules about acceptable classroom behavior. "Listen when others are talking." "Don't make fun of someone else's mistakes." However, some teachers are not kind when they talk to students. One 13-year-old told his mother, "The teachers are so mean. They tell us to show respect, but they yell at us and put kids down and order us around all day."

Some children are disrespectful because their parents don't place sufficient limits on inappropriate behavior. Parents may believe that rudeness is inevitable and they may excuse their child when she picks on unpopular classmates or calls them names. "Kids are cruel. They attack each other all the time."

At times, parents consciously or unconsciously encourage their child's disrespectful behavior. One boy loudly questioned a referee's call during a Little League game. The boy's father said, "Good. Somebody had to tell that guy off." That parental attitude can be seen almost anywhere there is competition: tennis matches, soccer fields, classrooms, neighborhood games.

If you'd like your child to show more respect, set limits and give frequent reminders. Let her know in a firm, clear way how she should behave. "I expect you to tell your sister what you feel without calling her names." "You may not speak to Dad and me so rudely. We'll listen if you change your tone." Show her the difference between thoughtless and respectful language. "Instead of calling Sara a pig, say, 'I'm angry at you for eating the candy. I wanted some.' "

When you see your child acting rudely, avoid giving an immediate lecture. She won't listen, but will only defend herself ("It wasn't my fault!") or talk back at you ("Leave me alone!"). Instead, give her a quiet suggestion or instruction. "You're being too harsh." "You need to be a better sport." "You shouldn't pick on a friend."

Later, when the incident has passed and you and your child are calmer, talk about what happened. The discussion may stir up feelings, so handle the subject delicately. First, listen to your child's defense and thoughts, then tell her what you've observed. "When you ask for something, you sound very demanding." Let your child know how important her tone and choice of words are. Ask her to imagine herself in another person's position.

Teaching your child to be respectful takes time, patience, and a lot of involvement. Eventually your lessons will get through and your child will learn to be respectful on her own.

How Can I
Encourage Discussion?

Good communication is a basic part of successful family life. Parents and children should talk to each other often about a whole range of subjects—school, friends, news events, hobbies, sports, politics, art, humor, science, music, religion, nature. The more children discuss at home, the more they learn about themselves and their world and prepare for adult life. Home is the best place for wide-ranging discussions, since schools often emphasize silence and order, and young peers have only limited information and perspectives. At home, a child can test out his ideas and start to think critically, analytically, and abstractly.

Discussions come more easily for some families than for others. Some parents never think of tossing ideas back and forth with their child. Other parents feel they don't have time to sit and talk. Children who aren't used to regular discussions rarely initiate conversations.

Most parents are greatly influenced by their own early experiences. If they grew up in families that valued talking, they talk often with their own children. One father remembers frequent discussions that turned into loud political debates. Although keeping up with his family was a constant challenge, this father believes he learned a great deal from those early talks. Another parent has very different memories. Throughout her childhood she had to listen silently to her parents' opinions. When she entered college, she froze if asked to speak in class. She'd had little experience sharing her ideas.

If you'd like your family to do more talking, set aside time for discussions. In the car, turn off the radio and start a conversation. Watch a little less TV, wake up twenty minutes early for a family breakfast, take an evening walk together, chat during dinner or over a late-night snack. If there are enough opportunities, you and your child will start talking.

Show your interest by asking your child questions. "What did you think of that movie?" "What's the best thing that happened today?" "What changes would you make at your school?" "If you were given money to help others, what would you do?" Share anecdotes about your day, describe articles from the newspaper, offer stories about your past or your child's early years, tell jokes. If your child is not used to discussions, let him do a lot of the talking. This will show you value his ideas and will enhance his self-esteem.

Don't overwhelm your child. In your eagerness to share information or insight, you may speak too long or too forcefully. Like most parents, you want to express your beliefs and shape your child's views. But if your child believes you will lecture to him or dismiss his words or start arguing, he may avoid family discussions. He's most likely to listen and respond if conversations are low-key.

It's important that you make the effort to talk with your child. At times it may be difficult to listen to his opinions or focus on his interests. Still, by talking to him you show the value of sharing ideas. From simple family conversations, he'll discover how to present himself, how to learn from others, and how to see the world from different viewpoints.

How Much Should
I Share About My
Personal Problems?

Every parent has problems. There are the relatively minor ones of daily life—overscheduling, errands, stressful commutes. There are chronic problems—job dissatisfaction, financial worries, conflicts in the extended family. And there are crises—impending divorce, job loss, serious illness, substance abuse. A difficult issue for all parents is deciding how much to tell their children about these problems.

Many parents want to shelter their child, thinking she has enough pressures of her own from school, peers, sports, and chores. They don't want to further burden her with parental problems she can't solve or fully understand. Besides, parents are often embarrassed by their own problems or worried that their child will spread personal information outside the family.

However, parents may remember their own early

feelings about family problems and secrets. One woman recalls having little information about her parents' arguments, but feeling worried and responsible. "They would yell and I would hide my head under the pillow, hoping the noise would go away." Some adults remember sneaking to overhear conversations and wishing their parents would reassure them. "I was scared when my father got so sick. I thought it was my fault."

It's difficult to keep serious problems from children. When something is wrong, children sense their parents' uneasy moods. They hear snatches of private phone calls and discussions. One 10-year-old whispered to a family friend who called, "My Mom can't talk now. Her mother is very sick, but she doesn't think I know." Some children hear angry outbursts. "I wish he'd stop drinking!" "Her whole family is crazy!"

During stressful times, children also experience differences in their parents' behavior, since a parent may be distracted or less patient about common annoyances. "Go do your homework in the other room!" "Stop making so much noise!" In the face of difficulties, some parents have a hard time controlling their emotions and actions. One mother, dealing with her husband's job loss, took her frustrations out on her 10- and 13-year-olds. She found fault with them and sometimes hit them, only to feel guilty about her lack of control. "My problems were so big, I couldn't even handle a question like 'Who's taking me to baseball practice?' "

The most common and upsetting adult problem children witness is marital stress. (See pps. 40–43, "How

Can I Help My Child Deal with Divorce?") When a child overhears arguments between her parents, she feels frightened, powerless, and worried. If she's not supposed to know about their conflict because they haven't told her, she can't ask questions or talk about her feelings. The problem may seem worse because she doesn't have information. Like most children, she may be quick to draw dreadful conclusions, blame herself, and fantasize about solutions. What a child wants most is reassurance, but she can't get it if her parents are secretive.

When deciding how much to tell your child, you have to consider many factors: your need for privacy, your level of comfort, your child's emotional makeup, and your child's desire—or lack of desire—for information. If you are an open person, you may not want to keep problems to yourself. If you are private, you may be too uncomfortable to share. If your child is mature and empathetic, it may be fine to tell her about some of your difficulties. But if she's not able to handle family problems, respect her wishes. One child, hearing of her parents' conflicts with relatives, said, "Don't tell me any more bad stories about Uncle Alex. They keep me from having fun when we go there." This child wanted to believe her family was happy and secure, and she felt overwhelmed by their conflicts.

It can take considerable energy to keep children from knowing about your personal problems. You will have to hold on to your thoughts and hide your feelings. Yet, at times, the effort involved may help you put your difficulties in perspective. "I only stopped worrying about our finances when I concentrated on my son and his activities."

Inevitably, there will be personal issues you want to or have to share with your child. Tell her as much as she needs to know—not all the details, but enough to open communication and give her a chance to ask questions. If you are having marital conflicts, let your child know about the general problem and make an effort to keep actual arguments private, behind closed doors.

When you tell your child about your difficulties, apologize when appropriate for losing your temper or not being available. Your child may understand, but don't expect her to feel as you do about your concerns or to offer solutions.

If communication is open without being overwhelming, your child will feel included. Just knowing she can talk will lessen her anxiety and make it easier for her to concentrate on school and her other activities. As you go through difficult times, she will see you handling hardships. She also will understand that problems don't have to be hidden and that it is all right to ask for help. Even though there are few easy answers, you want her to learn that talking about hard times is helpful and healing. Later, when she needs your advice about her own difficulties, she won't keep them to herself or worry that you can't handle them emotionally. She will have learned from your example that problems don't have to be secret.

My Child's View
of Adults Is Negative

"The principal is so strict." "Grown-ups think they know everything." "My coach doesn't put me in the game enough." "Adults always get in front of kids."

Many children complain about adults. They speak disparagingly of them, show them little respect, and shut them out. For some children, this negative view is an inevitable result of being young and dependent. For others, it is an adopted attitude, influenced by peers, TV, and movies. But for some children, it is a sign of troubling relationships with the adults around them.

At its simplest level, a negative view of adults comes from a child's sense of powerlessness. Parents, teachers, grandparents, coaches, and counselors have high expectations and often make harsh-sounding demands. "Clean up your room." "Stop talking during class." "Get over here." "Don't fight with your brother." "Be on time." Children, especially sensitive ones, are easily affected by an unkind tone or manner. They feel hurt, angry, or defensive, and react with skepticism and a broad generalization: "Adults are mean."

Negative attitudes are reinforced by peers and by the media. It may be "cool" to look down on adults. Since 10- to 13-year-olds are increasingly influenced by their friends, the attitude of one child may be copied by others. Many cartoons, sitcoms, and movies portray adults, especially parents, as bumbling, wrongheaded, or even evil. The more exposure children have to TV, the more they hear about incompetent, uncaring adults.

Of course, there are some uncaring adults, and the negative attitudes of some children are justified by the harsh treatment they've received. A child who feels threatened by the adults in his life will be angry and frustrated, and he may act in a belligerent way. Any child who lives in an atmosphere of mistrust and inflexibility will have a hard time being open and cooperative. Misbehaving may be the only way he has to release his hostility and give back what he receives.

If your child shows a superficial dislike for adults, explain how you feel about his attitude and set limits on his behavior. "I don't talk to you in a rude way, and I don't want you to be rude to me." "I want you to sound more respectful when you speak to your grandmother." To lessen the impact of negative influences, consider limiting TV time and talking to your child about his friends' attitudes.

If your child has a strong negative feeling toward adults, find out why. The cause may lie in the way he's treated at home. Ask yourself, "Am I too controlling? Do I offer my child choices or let him make decisions? Do I yell too much? Is my tone too angry? Do I compromise or listen enough? Am I a good role model?"

Let your child express his feelings. This may be hard for you and him if he hasn't had much chance to speak out. Because of pent-up emotions, he may say very negative things about adults in general and about you specifically. "You treat Jeffrey better than you treat me." "You're never home." "You always make me do what I don't want to do." "You're never happy with my report card." "You get too mad." "You never say I do a good job." As difficult as it is to listen to such words, it's important to take your child seriously. If necessary, use a timer so each of you can speak for five or ten uninterrupted minutes.

Once you know the causes of your child's negative attitude, both you and he will have to make changes. As a first step, give up unrealistic expectations for each other; there are no perfect children or parents. Show that you're willing to compromise and cooperate. This may include treating your child with more respect and changing some of the ways you act. Then set limits for your child, letting him know how you expect him to behave. As he makes changes, offer frequent encouragement. "I'm enjoying our relationship much more now." "Your attitude toward adults seems less negative." "I appreciate the way you've been acting." With patience and continuing effort, you and your child can achieve a common goal—a more trusting and harmonious family life.

FAMILY

LIFE

My Child Is Jealous
of Her Siblings

Every child feels some jealousy toward her siblings. A younger child resents an older one's abilities, privileges, and experience. A quiet child resents the attention her more outgoing or accomplished sibling receives. All children feel at least temporarily jealous of siblings who have received higher grades, newer shoes, more praise.

While some jealousy is inevitable, consistent jealousy comes from a child's belief that she's being treated unfairly, especially by her parents. Parents' attitudes and actions shape the relationships between siblings. A child may be right about her treatment, or she may be misreading her situation. But as long as she thinks she's being slighted, she'll be jealous.

Children are very sensitive to their parents' words. "My dad always says my brother's very smart." "They don't yell at her like they yell at me." "What's so great about Ben?" Parents at times give more positive attention to one child. Perhaps they feel that child needs encouragement or is temporarily vulnerable. "You did a terrific job on your spelling test!" They may feel proud of one child's accomplishments. "Show Grandma and Grandpa what you learned in ballet."

Sometimes without realizing it, parents favor one child. They may believe they're fair, but in subtle and powerful ways, they give great cause for jealousy. "Becky's very organized, but Stacey is so messy." "Matt is so much slower at homework than his brother." "Thank goodness Katie's such an easy child."

When children feel jealousy, whether justified or not, they may want to talk about it. "You always let her sit up front!" However, many parents get angry or won't listen. "That's nonsense!" "You have just as many things as your brother." If a child gets in trouble for protesting, she'll stop speaking up. If she believes she's hurt her parents, she'll also feel guilty for her negative thoughts about them. Complaining is too risky if it means making parents angry or losing their love. A child who can't express the truth or who doesn't fully understand her feelings will direct all her anger toward a safer person—her sibling—thereby reinforcing their rivalry.

Although family relationships are well established by the time a child is 10, there are constructive changes you can make if you want to lessen sibling rivalry. The most important is to listen, especially if jealousy between your children is significant. Have your children explain how they feel about your words and actions.

Let them say what disappoints them. You may find this difficult, but when problems are out in the open and discussable, change is more likely to happen. If your children don't raise the issue of jealousy but you believe it's a problem, initiate the discussion yourself.

Let your children know that you've heard them. "You're saying that things don't seem fair in this family." Listen to their suggestions. "I want you to tell me my work is good." "You and Dad should come to my games more." "Don't always talk about Ian."

Put limits on your children's rivalry. "While Mom and I are working on changes, we expect you to work on getting along better." Tell them you won't tolerate constant bickering. Sometimes children struggle with each other because they haven't been firmly told not to.

Honesty and openness will gradually enhance your children's relationship. When your jealous child feels heard and sees that changes are being made, she'll start to feel better about her siblings. During this time of change, you may want assistance from a third party such as a therapist or counselor. (See pps. 199–202, "Does My Child Need Therapy?") Even positive differences can be hard to accept or get used to.

While one of your children may be enjoying the attention you begin to give her, a previously "favored" child may have to adjust to a new situation. That child may have to learn to share your time and attention. Tell her, "We never realized your brother felt left out. We love you as much as always, but we're trying to be more fair now to both of you." You may find that your "favored" child is relieved to be out of the spotlight, just

25

as a teacher's pet may be glad to give up that title. It's often awkward for a child who receives better treatment than others.

Think about the ways your children's lives affect each other. As one child succeeds in school, another may need more attention. As one goes off with friends, the other may need support. Try to create a balance so that, despite differences in age, interests, personality, and skills, each of your children feels special and important.

Finally, encourage your children to be nice to each other. Praise their kind gestures, recognize the times they accept each other, and show them, by your words and actions, the benefits of harmonious family relationships.

Our Family Celebrations Are Changing

Celebrations and rituals are essential—they're part of the glue that keeps families together. Many holiday rituals, such as trick-or-treating or a visit to Santa, are aimed at young children. Other family traditions involve all the generations: Thanksgiving, the Fourth of July, the Passover Seder. In spite of the work involved, parents look forward to these annual celebrations as a time for family togetherness. But as children reach 10 to 13 years old, they may no longer want to participate in the same ways, if at all. Instead of being excited about an upcoming event, a 12-year-old may shock and disappoint his parents by asking, "Do I have to go?"

At these ages, children reject some family traditions because they are beginning to be self-conscious. A child may feel awkward about dressing up, playing games, and being in the spotlight. He wonders what others think of him. "Do I look stupid in this costume?" He may feel he's outgrown a celebration. "I'm too old for parades!" Because 11- to 13-year-olds are easily embarrassed, they may not want to be seen with their parents, especially if friends are around. "I don't want to go to the fireworks with you. I'd rather go with Gwen."

It's sad for parents when certain rituals end. Adults who've enjoyed decorating Easter eggs and hosting cake-and-ice-cream birthday parties don't want to give up the close times they've had with their children. A child's reluctance to participate in holidays reminds parents of his growing independence and inevitable separation from them.

Still, people of all ages need family traditions. If your child is beginning to reject your rituals, you can make some accommodations while still reinforcing the importance of celebrating together.

For example, try changing the way you mark a holiday. One mother who always decorated for Halloween didn't want to give up the tradition when her children became teenagers. Now she decorates only the hallway for trick-or-treaters to see, and her children, though perhaps "too old" for the holiday, like seeing the ritual continued.

Your child may feel better about family celebrations if you modify the circumstances a bit. Let him bring a friend along. Suggest that he take a Walkman or a book to a gathering; however, let him know he should spend most of his time socializing. Limit the amount of time you spend at family get-togethers. You will have fewer struggles if you bend a little.

Create new celebrations to mark the changes in your child's life. On the last day of school, go out to dinner. Finish the sport's season with a special lunch. One 10-year-old prompted her family to start an annual Kids' Day.

There are some holidays you won't want to change. If certain celebrations are very important, let your child know he has to take part. "We always go to midnight mass on Christmas eve." "You have to spend Passover with us at Aunt Susan's." In busy times these events bring your family together and give your family its identity. As your child grows, these annual celebrations will become the traditions he remembers and carries on.

We're Spending Less
Time Together

Families always seem to be busy. Parents' weekdays are filled with work, appointments, carpools, chores, errands, and volunteer projects. Weekends, rather than being relaxing, are times for shopping, driving to children's activities, laundry, household repairs, and paying bills.

Children's schedules are full too. In addition to school, homework, and chores, a 10- to 13-year-old may have lessons, classes, sports activities, or religious school. She may spend time talking on the phone, getting together with her friends, working on hobbies, reading, listening to music, watching TV, or playing video games. Between her activities and her parents', there's little time for the family to be together.

Eventually, this lack of closeness can lead to problems. Everyone knows older parents who say, "I wish

I'd spent more time with the kids when they were young." The parent-child relationship is built during childhood and adolescence, and once the time to be together on a daily basis passes—usually by age 18—parents can be left with many regrets.

You should make a special effort to be together with your child, even if you seem to have little opportunity or energy. By rearranging your schedule or giving up some of the things you now spend time on—socializing, volunteering, working long hours, keeping the house in perfect order—you can make yourself more available.

If your child wants to tell you a story, try putting down the paper or the mail and giving her your undivided attention. When she practices piano, occasionally sit with her and listen. When you're both in the car, use the time for discussion. Start having breakfast together or stay off the phone in the evenings so you and your child can talk.

The initiative has to come from you because your child may be too busy or self-absorbed to think about your lack of time together. While it's natural for her to want to be with friends much of the day, make it clear that family time—whether regularly planned or spontaneous—is important too. One way around conflicts is to include her friends in some of your family activities.

When you focus on your child's interests, she will welcome your increased attention. You can sit in her room while she talks about her day or you can listen to music together. You may be surprised to find that you and she like some of the same kinds of songs. Try

31

playing a board game or video game together, making dessert, reading out loud, or sitting at the kitchen table with a cup of hot chocolate.

Try not to use your limited time together to reprimand your child. In some families, the only time parents and children talk is to argue. While it's important to settle disagreements, the calm and enjoyable hours you spend together are valuable. They help create an atmosphere that makes it easier for your child to be cooperative and open.

This is a period of rapid changes for your child. One father realized with a shock that in only four years his 13-year-old would be off to college. "I don't have much time left with him." The everyday events that fill your calendar should not keep you from spending time with your child as she grows and matures. Sharing good times is an important part of strengthening the bond between you.

"I Just Want
Some Privacy!"

"Leave me alone!" "I want to be by myself."

As children get older, their desire for privacy increases. Ten and 11-year-olds like occasional time alone, but many 12- and 13-year-olds spend considerable time by themselves. This is a natural consequence of their growing independence; however, some parents find it troubling. "It doesn't seem right when my daughter goes off to her room. It feels like she's rejecting the whole family." Parents remember how their young child used to follow them and how he felt most comfortable and secure when they were close by. They may wonder why he now wants to spend so much time on his own.

Children often go into their bedrooms and shut the door because they want to relax in a quiet atmosphere. Some read, listen to music, draw, or organize baseball cards. Some enjoy private time in a room with a video game, TV, or telephone. By going off by themselves, children are able to get away from the stresses and noise of younger siblings and household activities.

Children also seek privacy to get away from adult demands. After a day spent with teachers and coaches, parents' questions and expectations can seem overwhelming. And in some families, when a child is in sight, he's given spontaneous chores. "As long as you're in the kitchen, please set the table." "Take Katie out to play." "Help me straighten the family room." A child learns that if he goes right to his room, he's less likely to receive added responsibilities.

In some cases, a child may isolate himself in an attempt to escape from problems. He may be having trouble making friends or keeping up with schoolwork. He may also be retreating from family conflicts. Time alone can offer a short reprieve from difficulties, but parents should be concerned if their child consistently shows signs of depression, such as eating less, sleeping more, losing interest in friends and activities, moping, or appearing sad or angry.

If you're worried about your child's excessive desire for privacy, talk to him about your concerns. You may discover that he goes to his room out of habit, and your reminders may be enough to change his behavior. You may learn that he's upset about school and homework or that he feels pressured by responsibilities or arguments at home. Try to decrease his stress—offer help with assignments, time with a tutor, fewer demands. Also provide encouragement and positive attention.

As long as your child's time alone is not excessive, respect his wish for privacy and, if necessary, help him out. Ask younger siblings to keep their distance for a short while. Allow him free time during the day. If your children share a bedroom, have them work out a schedule for time alone or let your 10- to 13-year-old spend periods by himself in another room. If you allow your child adequate privacy, he'll willingly balance that by spending time with family and friends.

My Child Thinks

I'm an Embarrassment

"**D**on't come in when you pick me up at school."
"Please don't be a chaperone." "We can't go to the mall
together—my friends might be there."

Twelve- and 13-year-olds are easily embarrassed by
their parents. They may feel humiliated by anything
their parents do in public: laugh out loud, cheer at a
game, sneeze, wave, or simply stand around. Parents
may put up with their child's embarrassment and may
even be amused by it for a while. But sometimes they
find it annoying to be warned off, criticized, and
ignored.

A child this age is self-conscious and uncertain about
her own behavior. She can easily extend her own self-
consciousness to include her parents' behavior, feeling
that what they do reflects on her. If her parents "make

a mistake," the child worries that her friends will think less of her. One father, out with his son, said "Hi Andy" to a child whose name was really Annie. Annie didn't mind, but the son was extremely embarrassed. "When you said the wrong name it made me feel dumb."

Being part of the group is very important to 12- and 13-year-olds. They are becoming increasingly independent of their parents and want to spend more time with their peers. A child wants to act the way her friends do, which is different from the way she acts at home. When her friends and her parents are together, even briefly, the child feels embarrassed and awkward. She doesn't want her parents to see her joke around and relate to her peers, especially those of the opposite sex. And she doesn't want her friends to see how she behaves with her family. One child was invited to a bar mitzvah along with her parents. She told them, "I'm not going to like this. I can't dance if you're there looking at me."

A child cares a great deal about her friends' opinions, including their opinion of her parents. It's hard to convince her that her peers are emotionally removed from all parents but their own. She still feels that her parents are the focus of attention. And even if her parents are young in spirit, have a good relationship with her, and are comfortable with her friends, she will continue to worry.

You may think your child's embarrassment is silly. But she is showing common early adolescent thinking and behavior. You can probably remember similar feelings about your own parents. One mother told her grown daughter, "You used to be just like Erica is. You always wanted me to walk three feet in front of you." If you and your child discuss the issue honestly, you will probably hear that she likes being with you at home or at activities where parents are usually involved, such as watching a game or eating out. She just doesn't want to be with you in front of her friends.

You can try modifying some of your behavior to show respect for your child's feelings. If she doesn't want you to tell jokes or act silly when her friends are present, go along with her. However, if her embarrassment is consistently excessive, let her know you will have to be together in public at times. You should continue to talk to her friends when you see them.

Don't try to lessen your child's embarrassment by becoming "friends" with her and her peers. Dressing, talking, or behaving like an adolescent is not appropriate. Your child needs to feel separate from you. Work on building a positive relationship with her by talking, showing an interest, guiding her, and respecting her.

While the majority of children feel embarrassment over minor incidents, some have to deal with seriously embarrassing situations involving irresponsible parents or parents who are alcoholics or drug users. If your family is experiencing complex problems, your child—and the rest of the family—can benefit from professional help. (See pps. 199–202, "Does My Child Need Therapy?")

In most cases, however, embarrassment is short-lived and nothing to worry about. Once your child gains more independence and experience socializing, her embarrassment will fade and her comfort with you will increase.

How Can I Help
My Child Deal
with Divorce?

Parents don't want the breakup of their marriage to harm their child. Before divorce, many parents seek advice from a family therapist about minimizing their child's suffering. During and after the divorce, most parents' love and concern for their child remains unchanged. Yet the stress of divorce can be so intense that parents eventually find it hard to keep concentrating on their child's needs.

Divorce can be devastating for children. Many parents want to believe their child will "bounce back." "Kids are so resilient." "He'll get over it after a little while." But children don't easily recover. Some may seem unaffected simply because they have busy schedules and many distractions. Others keep their feelings to themselves for fear of further upsetting or angering their parents. A child who is confused, ashamed, or embarrassed may hide or deny his feelings rather than talk about this tough issue. And many emotions are repressed.

What a child of divorce usually feels is sadness, anger, hurt, and sometimes a sense of abandonment. Even if he was exposed to frequent turmoil when his parents were together, he usually won't greet the divorce with relief. Almost all children want their family to stay together, and they feel powerless when they can't make their wish come true. One 12-year-old whose parents had been separated for a year told her friend, "For my birthday I don't want any presents. I just want my family to have dinner together again." A 10-year-old wrote a note to a classmate: "You're always happy. Is that because your parents aren't divorced?"

After divorce, a child is often expected to behave more maturely than before, take care of himself, assume some of the absent parent's responsibilities, or provide emotional support to the parent at home. These are impossible burdens for any child who finds the condition of his family life and the state of his childhood dramatically changed.

Even the most comfortable parts of a child's life may suddenly become stressful after divorce. Dinner and bedtime may be awkward. Family celebrations may be uncomfortable and relationships with grandparents, aunts, uncles, and cousins may be strained or even cut off.

If parents are very angry about the divorce, all aspects of a child's everyday life will be affected. Some parents may coerce their child into taking sides, leaving him feeling guilty and resentful. If he does blame one parent for the breakup, he may idealize the other one, praising him or her in the presence of the "bad" parent.

All these potentially negative experiences and feelings, if not dealt with carefully by parents, can cause great emotional harm. A child may develop a poor self-image, distrust, a pessimistic outlook, or depression. He may also have trouble in school or with peers and siblings.

If a child is going to get through a divorce without such emotional difficulties, parents have to commit themselves to putting his needs first—to consistently giving love and attention and being deeply involved in his life. He needs extra affection and understanding during and after a breakup, and he needs both of his parents to be nurturers and role models.

Parents have to refrain from speaking ill of each other in their child's presence. The parent who does not live with the child has to have frequent contact, drive carpools, go to the child's special events, and help with homework. If a parent does not stay involved, the child will feel rejected and unworthy of love.

To help your child through divorce, encourage him to talk. Let him know he can share his worries, anger, and questions. You'll find out what he's thinking and you can clear up confusion. "No, we aren't going to move. We're staying right here in our house."

Offer information and answer your child's questions. He'll want to know about changes. Will he still go on vacations and visit relatives? Where will his father live? Will you start dating? What should he tell his friends?

Who will he celebrate holidays with? You should raise these issues if your child doesn't bring them up. He'll feel less worried knowing you and he can talk openly.

Don't expect too much from your child. He won't be any better at making decisions or being responsible than he was before your divorce. He's still a child and his needs should come before yours or your ex-spouse's. If the practical side of parenting seems overwhelming, simplify your life to make more time for your child. Have easy meals, let some housekeeping chores go, cut back on outside commitments.

Encourage your child to stay in touch with your ex-spouse's relatives. Continuing his relationship with grandparents and cousins will help him feel part of an extended family.

Eventually your child will begin to understand and accept his situation, especially if he sees that neither of his parents is falling apart. He'll always wish there had never been a divorce. But he may appreciate the calmness that often follows the breakup of a troubled marriage. In time, with both natural parents' love and involvement, he should adjust to his new family structure.

I'm a Single Parent—
What About Dating?

It's common for children to have a hard time when their single parent begins to date. They may complain, sulk, or otherwise act out their discomfort and unhappiness. One child told her mother, "When you go out with a man, it's worse than the divorce!" Another child cried whenever she saw either of her parents with a new companion.

Parents who are excited about resuming their social lives may resent this display of anger and sadness. "Don't ruin things. I need a life too. It's not my fault your father left me." While parents can understand some of their child's unhappiness, they're often surprised by the depth of her negative feelings.

Most children resent their parents' dating because they believe it makes a family reconciliation less likely. Ten- to 13-year-olds may still think they can bring their parents back together. A child may act rudely to her parents' dates in hopes of discouraging relationships outside the original family.

A child may also worry about receiving less attention once her parents begin dating. In a sense she feels abandoned as her single parent focuses time and energy on a new companion. A date is an intruder and a threat.

Sometimes a child remains distant toward her parents' dates because she fears involvement. "I think this guy will walk out on us like my dad did." The child doesn't want her mother to get hurt; she doesn't want to get hurt herself. If her father begins dating, a child may have the same worries about him, or—depending on the circumstances of her parents' divorce—she may fear that he won't be loyal to his new companion.

Finally, a child may be uncomfortable with her parents' social life because she herself is becoming interested in dating. Twelve- and 13-year-olds who are discovering their own sexual and romantic feelings dislike imagining that their parents have similar thoughts.

To deal with your child's worries, keep the lines of communication open when you start dating. Find out what your child thinks, even if you'd rather not know. She'll feel better talking openly about her concerns. Acknowledge your difficulties. "This is awkward, isn't it?" Ask, "How can I help you feel better about my dating?" Imagine yourself in your child's place—it might help you understand her and be more patient.

When you first date someone, try meeting him or her at a location other than your home. There's no point in upsetting your child by having her greet everyone you go out with—introduce her only to those dates you'll continue seeing.

Before bringing dates home, tell them about your child and offer advice on dealing with her. If your dates seem overly friendly, your child may withdraw. Brief, casual contact is best. If dates show a genuine interest in your child, she may respond favorably, although she may not want to spend much time with them. If dates compliment you or act affectionate in her presence, she may feel threatened and worry about losing you.

Deciding whether dates should spend the night when your child is home is an awkward part of dating. You can be matter-of-fact about a date's presence. "Bill's spending the night here." Or you can acknowledge the fact only if your child asks. If the situation becomes very stressful for your child, reevaluate your actions. You may decide to spend the night with a date only when your child is away. As you consider this difficult issue, remember that you're a role model for your child. Whatever your behavior, she may eventually copy it.

As you continue to date, you may be tempted to ask your child for acceptance or even advice. But don't expect too much from her. She won't be able to understand or validate your social life. She is more likely to be uncooperative, since she'd prefer that you didn't go out. If your expectations are unrealistic, you'll only become frustrated and angry.

You'll have to work hard at helping your child adjust. The more time you spend talking with her, being with her, and building a positive relationship, the easier her adjustment will be. If your dating takes too much time and attention away from her, you and she will be in conflict. If your child has unusual difficulty with your dating, she may need extra support. Therapy groups can focus on her fears and help her accept the realities of her life with you.

We're Trying to Adjust to Our Blended Family

All families have to work at living in harmony. Blended families, especially ones with 10- to 13-year-olds, have to try particularly hard. Children these ages go through tremendous physical and emotional changes as they form their adolescent identities. In the midst of their internal upheavals, they may react quite negatively to a new stepfamily. And new stepparents may have negative feelings of their own. They rarely feel the same bond with a stepchild that they do with their natural children. Adjusting to life in a blended family requires much commitment, patience, and understanding from all members.

Parents may have an easier time if they understand the child's point of view. If he's still sad about his parents' divorce or feels abandoned by one of his parents, a child may fear attachment to another adult who might leave. He may also worry about losing the love and attention of his newly married parent, seeing the step-parent as an intruder and rival.

The stepparent is another authority figure, and a pre- or early adolescent will resent new or different rules and restrictions. The child doesn't want his natural parent to give up control. "If he didn't live with us, you wouldn't make me clean my room so much!" "Why do I have to go to bed early just because Margaret said so?"

When a stepparent joins a family, many rituals and routines change, and a 10- to 13-year-old child finds that upsetting. He doesn't want his natural parent to act differently, and he doesn't want to alter the patterns of everyday life.

A child who resents a stepparent may act on his feelings in a number of ways. He may try to sabotage the new marriage by being intentionally uncooperative and belligerent. He may fantasize that his actions will bring his natural parents together again.

The child may use his stepparent as a target for all his frustration and anger. "It's Jim's fault I didn't do well on the test. I can't study when he's around." "It's never fun going out to dinner anymore because of Ellen and her dumb kids." He feels safe doing this because he has little to lose: He doesn't care what his stepparent thinks of him.

One reason a child may focus so much blame on the stepparent is because he wants his natural parent to be the "good" one. If he gets upset at him or her, he risks feeling guilty, losing his parent's love, and facing his parent's anger.

Another complication in blended families is the presence of stepsiblings. At these ages, children don't want to be told whom to like. Yet in a blended family they're thrown together with new siblings and forced to socialize, have their weekends interrupted by visits from each other, share possessions and perhaps even a bedroom, and compete for attention from parents. It's natural that stepsiblings feel resentment about perceived unfairness. And if the parents in a remarriage have different discipline standards, stepsiblings will argue about who has to listen to which adult.

Yet in spite of the difficulties, blended families can be successful. To help your family during its adjustment, look for stepfamily social or support groups in your area. These groups offer an opportunity to talk about concerns, hear tips on getting along, and listen to other families' experiences. You might also consider using a therapist to help improve your family's relationships.

Talk often at home. Hold family meetings, allowing each member to speak without interruption about troubling issues. To avoid angry outbursts, set ground rules—no put-downs or criticism and no yelling. Such meetings can create a positive family atmosphere and clear up misunderstandings.

If you are a stepparent, be patient as you get to know your stepchild. Ask him about his activities and interests, go to his games, and help him with his hobbies. Don't create or enforce rules unless you have a good relationship with him, and don't try to replace his absent natural parent. If he rejects you, look for possible openings. Will he let you help with homework? Can you play tennis, cook, bike, garden, sing, or read together?

If you're the natural parent, spend time alone with your child, reinforcing your relationship. Praise him if he tries to get along with his stepfamily. "I know it's hard sometimes. Thanks for trying." Be realistic in your expectations for the relationship between your spouse and your child. Tell your child how you'd like him to act and remind him, if necessary, that disrespectful behavior is not acceptable. "We don't treat you that way and we don't want you treating us that way." Take on the role of disciplinarian for your child, rather than leaving that responsibility to your spouse.

Be sensitive to the difficulty stepsiblings have with their new arrangements. It takes time for children to adjust to each other. Ask them for suggestions about getting along and dealing with conflicts.

As you adjust to your blended family, it's important that your marriage remain loving and stable. Remarriages are often difficult, and stepfamily tension coupled with everyday stress can be very disruptive. If you put time and effort into your relationship with your spouse, you will not only strengthen the bonds of your marriage, but your bonds with your child as well. When he sees that you love and enjoy each other, he may try harder to accept his situation. And he may realize that his anger and stubbornness are causing him to miss out on a satisfying family life.

CHANGES

My Child Is
So Moody

"**A**ll I did was ask about the party and my daughter started crying." "Every day my son comes home from school in a lousy mood." "Why does my child get so angry when plans change?" "Where did I go wrong?"

Emotions during the pre- and early adolescent years are intense and unpredictable. One moment a child feels rage and the next seems calm and delightful. Mood changes and bursts of temper often take parents by surprise. A simple question asked of a 13-year-old ("Do you think that sweater will keep you warm?") can solicit a furious response. "Mom, you just don't understand anything. I hate talking to you!" One 11-year-old instantly went from happy to belligerent when his mother ran a brief errand on the way to baseball practice. "Why do you always have to stop at stores?" A

12-year-old left for school in a bad mood because she was out of hair spray.

Everyone feels moody at times; emotional ups and downs are a normal part of life, but they're exaggerated for 10- to 13-year-olds. During these years, children go through great physical, intellectual, and psychological changes, all of which affect their emotions. A child begins to think about her beliefs and values. She becomes capable of considering other people's thoughts and opinions. Unfortunately, she often assumes people are thinking about her, especially in critical ways. She may act very self-consciously. "Will my freckles go away?" "Why is everyone staring at me?" "I wanted to die when I tripped up the steps at school." She may feel inferior to her peers. "Why am I the one with horrible hair?" Such insecurity causes frequent mood swings.

As part of the normal drive for independence at these ages, a child distances herself from her parents and in the process becomes more critical of their actions and choices. A child can imagine an ideal self and family. When she or her parents fall short, she can easily become unhappy or angry.

In addition, thoughts and emotions that were suppressed or not easily verbalized during earlier years might surface now. A child may become very upset about unfair treatment in the past. "You're always so critical. I can't be perfect!" Through bad moods and angry outbursts, she releases her frustration with her parents.

There is another reason for mood swings: Life gets

more complex and stressful for children at these ages. Competitive sports, the move toward middle school, expanding social life, overscheduling, family conflicts, and worries about the world outside the home all affect a child's emotions. Parents' expectations also increase as children get older. One 13-year-old said, "Parents get their kids in bad moods. They order us to clean up, go somewhere, do something, and they ground us if we don't listen."

These are some of the underlying causes of mood swings. And almost any event can trigger a short temper or bad mood—a low grade on a test, a teasing remark, a disagreement with a friend or sibling, any embarrassment. If a child isn't invited to join her classmates after school, she may come home and shout at her brother. A boy who is criticized during gym class may in turn criticize his parents' choice of conversation at dinner.

Because many of the changes in a child's life are not experienced on a conscious level or are subtle, a pre- or early adolescent may be puzzled or upset by her own shifting moods. "I don't know why, but I'm depressed." "What's wrong with me?" "I'm sorry I get mad all the time." There's so much to sort through and understand that children sometimes feel out of control.

You can help your child feel less confused by telling him what you think is causing his anger. "You didn't expect to do poorly on the math test, did you?" "That was a tough game." "Brooke should have invited you too." Share experiences from your youth. "I remember how awful it felt not having someone to talk to at the bus stop." "I used to dump on Aunt Joanie a lot when I was in a bad mood."

Resist asking frequently "What's wrong?" or "Are you all right?" because your child will eventually react defensively. One 12-year-old told her mother, "I hate when you ask me if I'm in a bad mood."

While you should allow your child the occasional harmless outburst—everyone needs to let out some frustration—in general, don't accept rude, disrespectful behavior. Tell your child when her words are inappropriate; she might not view her moodiness or short temper in negative ways. "I'm really bothered by your tone." "You need to control your temper." Let her know the consequences of her behavior: the loss of privileges, time in her room.

Examine and, if necessary, change your own behavior. If you have a short temper or frequently act moody, your child may be copying you. Think about circumstances that might be exaggerating your child's moodiness, such as difficulty with schoolwork, tension at home, or excessive pressure to excel. If you can ease some of these problems and bolster your child's self-confidence in any way, you'll see an improvement in her temperament. One child began to feel calmer when his parents let him drop out of competitive swimming.

When your child is pleasant or cooperative, compliment her. In general, tell her she's a "good kid." And try to have a sense of humor in the face of normal pre-teen and early adolescent behavior. One parent told his 13-year-old, "Stop acting like a 13-year-old!"

Your child, like most, probably saves her short temper and moodiness for home, where she feels relatively safe and secure. At school, with friends, and with adults other than her parents she's most likely polite and controlled. Moodiness at home is a normal part of development. Try to be loving, supportive, and patient.

I'm Tired of Reminding My Child to Use Deodorant

One of the earliest signs of puberty is increased body odor. In the beginning, it may only be detectable after a child finishes playing a sport or participating in gym class. As the child gets older, the need for deodorant becomes more obvious.

Children sometimes hear about body odor from teachers who discuss general hygiene in class. Sometimes they hear about it from classmates. "You have b.o." "Jeremy stinks!" More often, however, children won't mention body odor to a friend for fear of hurting his feelings. Instead, it's a parent who first tells a child to start using deodorant.

The child's reaction will vary, depending on his maturity and his ability to practice good hygiene. Some children are quite practical. They are independent about getting ready for school and activities, and they easily incorporate deodorant use into their daily routine with only an occasional reminder.

Many other 10- to 13-year-olds need frequent reminders. These children have much on their minds, especially in the morning. "Where's my lunch money? Did I study enough for the math test? What pants should I wear? I wish I could go back to sleep." They have trouble remembering about teeth, cleanliness, and nails, and deodorant is just one more thing that's easily forgotten.

Finally, some children these ages may not yet be ready—or willing—to think about bodily changes, especially increased odor. They don't yet have an adolescent's concern about image, and they can't easily detect the odor themselves. They would just as soon ignore the issue.

This is frustrating for parents who want to spare their child and themselves embarrassment. They don't want their child to be teased and they don't want other adults to say, "He shouldn't let his kid smell like that." One teacher announced to her class, "Somebody in here has body odor."

To encourage your child to use deodorant, make it easy for him. Put the container in clear sight, along with his toothbrush, soap, and hairbrush. If deodorant is kept in a cabinet, your child may never think about it. Post a friendly or humorous note on the bathroom mirror. Gently remind him every morning. Put deodorant in his overnight bag when he sleeps out.

Don't let deodorant use become a source of conflict or power struggles. The issue is not important enough.

New routines always take time to learn, and soon enough your child will take over responsibility for this and the other aspects of grooming. The closer he gets to adolescence, the more he will focus on his body and his appearance.

For now, he's not being neglectful or lazy. He is either genuinely forgetting about deodorant or he is uncomfortable about this new part of his life. Let him know that his feelings are common, and keep talking to him about the importance of good hygiene.

How Can I Help My Child During Puberty?

Puberty is a time of exciting growth and change for children, and it's also a time of stress. Children have worries and questions about their bodies. They become increasingly private. They're concerned about their social lives and they're starting to distance themselves from their families. Parents are often unsure of how to deal with all the issues raised during this period.

One cause of concern for many children is the difference in rates of development. The desire to be like their peers is so strong that pre- and early adolescents who are maturing slowly may become upset and jealous. "When am I ever going to grow?" "Everybody treats me like I'm so young." A child who matures quickly may feel awkward and embarrassed. "People act like I'm already a teenager."

Girls are often self-conscious about their developing

breasts. "I'm wearing a T-shirt over my bathing suit." Because this aspect of puberty is so obvious, friends or classmates may tease a girl about her breast size. Some younger girls who develop early don't want to wear bras. The process of shopping in a lingerie department may be too intimidating for a child who feels modest.

Another issue of puberty is when to shave body hair. Girls—usually by age 12—are shaving their legs and underarms, and many boys are shaving off a mustache by 13. But some girls want to shave at a much earlier age, and some 12- and 13-year-old boys don't seem ready to shave, even if they have dark facial hair. "Why do I have to shave and my friends don't?" Parents and children may end up arguing about this aspect of personal hygiene.

Just as many families are uncomfortable discussing sex, they are also reluctant to talk about puberty. A child may mention her worries about height, but she may be too embarrassed to share her fear of being flat-chested. A boy can talk about the changes in his voice, but he won't ask his parents how much bigger his penis will get.

Parents may sense this self-consciousness; they may also feel reluctant to open a discussion about their child's body. Parents are often startled by the "sudden" changes they see, and they're curious about the changes they don't see. Yet it rarely feels appropriate to ask a child personal questions about her body.

Even if conversations about puberty seem awkward, let your child know she can ask you anything and that you'll be happy to talk whenever she wants. Offer her books and articles on puberty and treat her concerns and questions with respect. "I know you get embarrassed when we talk about sex. I do too. But I think you must be curious about it. Why don't we talk for a little while?" "It's been a few weeks since I gave you that book about puberty. What did you think of it?"

Give your child frequent compliments. "You're a terrific kid!" "You look great all dressed up." "It was really nice of you to help Grandpa paint his kitchen." Show that you love her no matter what changes she's going through.

If you think your child is focusing on her body too much, try to involve her in more activities and talk about her interests and accomplishments. "I love to hear you practice guitar." "What's your book about?" "Your painting for art class was beautiful."

Give your child practical help. If she's embarrassed about buying bras, bring some home from the store for her or let her go into the dressing room alone. If she develops pimples, find appropriate soaps or creams and, if necessary, take her to a dermatologist.

Talk to your daughter about menstruation so she knows what to expect. As long as she understands the basic facts, you can wait until she gets her period to discuss details such as pads, tampons, cramps, and irregular cycles. When she does begin menstruating, talk to her about her feelings and about such practical issues as changing pads at school and handling accidents. You should discreetly let her siblings know that their sister has started menstruating. Be careful when you do this. You don't want your other children to become alarmed if they see a used pad, but you also don't want to violate your daughter's sense of privacy.

If your child is maturing more quickly or slowly than average, keep treating her in a way that's appropriate for her chronological age. An 11-year-old who looks quite mature is still 11. Some parents make the mistake of letting their older-looking pre-teen wear makeup, dress more maturely, and go places without supervision. Similarly, parents of a more slowly developing child may tease her or treat her like a much younger person. "Are we always going to be shopping in the pre-teen department?"

Throughout puberty, your child will be especially vulnerable. Try to be patient and understanding. In the face of changes, she needs to know you love and accept her. The more support and encouragement you give, the better she'll feel about herself and her body.

What Do I Say
About Sex?

During a school meeting on pre-adolescent behavior, parents were asked to write down the one subject that was most difficult to discuss with their child. One mother was too embarrassed to write "sex," so she put down "homework." She later found out her friends had done the same thing. "They wrote 'chores,' 'talking back,' 'sibling rivalry'—anything but 'sex.'"

Most parents and children have a hard time talking to each other about sex. Parents find it difficult to imagine their child as a sexual being, and they're ambivalent about giving detailed information. Discussions often become embarrassing as parents blush and children try to change the subject. "Okay! I know about that. Let's not talk about it anymore."

Pre- and early adolescents are definitely interested in sex. They just don't want to discuss it with a parent.

"I'm not going to tell my father what I'm thinking about some girl." As a result, they look for information from peers, older siblings, books, TV, movies, and magazines. Some of what they find out is accurate, some is not. They rarely hear a discussion of values from these nonparental sources.

Most parents believe they should talk more about sex to their child than they do. They remember their own lack of knowledge as pre-teens and want their child to grow up in a more communicative home.

When children are young, parents have a relatively easy time telling them the basics of intercourse and childbirth. Yet as children approach adolescence, parents avoid discussions about the details: wet dreams, sexual arousal, masturbation. . . . "I'll wait a little while." "They talk about that in health class." "He's probably heard a lot already." Avoidance is not surprising. Adults rarely speak seriously about sex with anyone, even close friends.

As uncomfortable as you may be, try to find a workable way to communicate information and values to your child. If you want to discuss an aspect of sexuality, acknowledge your discomfort. "I feel really awkward, but there's something I want to tell you about." "I was too embarrassed to talk about this before, but I want to try now."

Briefly share your information. If your child wants to learn more, continue. If he doesn't, don't force a longer discussion. He may be more open if you talk about your own lack of information as a child. "When I was a kid, I pretended I knew what all the dirty words meant, but

I didn't. Do you hear words you don't understand?" Don't be surprised by blunt responses and questions. "Was Dad the first man you had sex with?" "What does 69 mean?"

As you briefly discuss different topics, include some of your personal thoughts on relationships and intimacy. Some parents clearly believe their child should abstain from intercourse until marriage; other parents take a more flexible approach; many parents don't know what advice to give. Whatever your position or degree of certainty, you can talk to your child about responsibility to himself and others, about "safe sex," and about loving relationships.

If discussing sex is too difficult for you, give your child one of the many good books on the subject, written for his age and maturity level. (See pps. 203–204, "Suggestions for Further Reading.") Urge him to read it, and offer to answer any questions he has. He will get the information he needs now, and you will still have opportunities in the future to talk about sexuality and values.

"DO I
LOOK OKAY?"

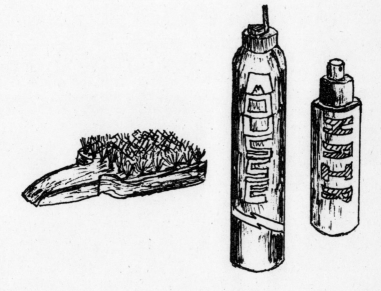

My Child and I
Have Different
Tastes in Clothes
and Hairstyles

As children get older, they want more control over clothing purchases and haircuts. Depending on age and interest, they may ask for a little more say or they may ask to make all decisions themselves. As long as parents and children share the same taste, there's usually little conflict. But when tastes differ, as they often do, there can be frequent struggles. Some parents first deal with this issue when their child is 10 to 12 years old; other parents have been arguing about clothes since their child was in preschool.

Most children decide how they want to look based on how their friends look. Dressing like a friend gives a child a sense of belonging; specific styles are less important than "fitting in." Some groups of children like clothes and hairstyles that draw attention. They want to wear outrageous shirts, turn a sweater inside out, or shave part of their hair. Some groups dress for comfort or prefer a conservative look. Still others are label conscious and like the latest fashions.

Under the influence of peers, a child may quickly change her mind about what she likes. One 11-year-old refused to wear the jacket her mother handed her. But when the girl's friend said "I like that coat," the girl put it on. Another child pleaded with his mother to buy a pair of decorated jeans. After wearing them to school one day, he said he'd never wear them again because everybody teased him. "I was so embarrassed I didn't want to stand up the whole day!"

Even without peer influence, a child's taste can suddenly change. She may get dressed for an occasion, look in the mirror, and say, "This dress is too big." "I like the pants but I don't like the shirt it came with." "I look terrible." She may think everything looks better on someone else. She may like her friends' clothes better than her own, even when the items are almost identical. Some children even exchange clothes with friends in school bathrooms.

All of this can be very frustrating for parents. Their suggestions are often ignored and their purchases rejected. "Mom, nobody wears that." Their advice is met with defensiveness. One parent told her 12-year-old daughter she dressed too much like a boy. Her daughter said, "But all my friends have these shirts!" One boy who got a stylish haircut over the objections of his parents said, "Now I look like a normal 13-year-old."

A child's desire for faddish or inappropriate clothes and hairstyles can easily lead to tension and arguments.

Some families struggle constantly over makeup, shaved heads, pierced ears, ripped jeans, and long bangs.

If you're unhappy about your child's taste, it's appropriate to set limits. Let her know she can't wear shirts with graphics or slogans you find offensive. Tell her which styles you won't allow. "Those earrings are too large." "Find a way to keep your hair out of your eyes." "That makeup is too harsh."

Try compromising on items that are acceptable but make you uncomfortable. "You can buy baggy jeans, but those are too large." "We can look for that shoe in another color." Let your child know when she can wear certain clothes. "Those shorts are fine if you're with your friends, but I want you to wear something neater to Uncle Alan's." If a major family event such as Thanksgiving is approaching, tell your child she'll have to wait until afterward to change her hairstyle.

While it's appropriate to set limits on extreme styles, try to accept many of your child's choices and compliment her as often as you can. She still wants your approval, and constant criticism from you can harm her self-image. Remember your own feelings about clothes, appearance, and independence while growing up. Your frustrations then are similar to your child's now.

You may find tensions decrease if you give your child a clothing allowance, as many parents of 13-year-olds do. Go over spending guidelines. "Use this money to buy one shirt and one pair of pants." "You can get one shirt for thirty dollars or two for thirty dollars, depending on which store you go to." Then let her shop with a friend.

Whatever your differences in taste, try to keep the issue in perspective. As long as your child does well in school, has friends, and is active and involved in activities, the style of haircut and clothing she prefers is relatively unimportant. The only need for concern is if your child isn't generally doing well and seems to choose styles to antagonize you. This may be the sign of a deeper problem you need to pay attention to.

How Should I
Handle Fads?

All children are attracted by fads and want at least some of the latest, short-lived styles in music, haircuts, clothes, gadgets, or games. At the beginning of the school year, children may be "tight-rolling" their pants. Two months later, a sixth-grader says, "Nobody does that anymore. Now they wear their pants long." A rock group that a girl has idolized may be quickly forgotten. A sports hat that a boy wants may soon end up in the closet.

Fads are popular because children want to be like their peers. If enough children have a particular object, others want it too, since no one wants to feel left out. In the same way, younger siblings desire what their older brothers and sisters have. Children are also heavily influenced by television commercials and magazine ads. Just as young children want the toys they see on

TV, 10- to 13-year-olds think that much of what is advertised for them looks wonderful.

Of course, adults can be attracted to fads of their own. But most adults know which styles will last awhile and which will quickly vanish. Children don't distinguish in the same ways. A child wants a gadget because it's appealing now; he's not thinking about its value or looking ahead.

That difference in perspective causes tension when parents discuss fads with their child. A parent may feel that a particular fad is too expensive or a waste of money. "I'm not paying that much for cheap-looking jewelry." Parents may disapprove of a fad or be completely against it. "That band sounds terrible—how can you listen to such junk?" "You're too young. You can't wear that makeup." "You may not pierce your ear."

Many parents try to reason with their child. "You shouldn't believe what you see on TV." "It's better to think for yourself." "You don't have to have something just because other kids do." But what appears silly or wasteful to a parent may be important and fashionable to a child. That's why children react defensively when their parents dismiss their requests. "You don't understand!" A child feels frustrated because, unlike an adult, he can't buy something simply because it attracts him. He needs approval, permission, and money, and he often has to listen to a lecture.

When your child wants something badly, hear him out. Don't label his request "just a fad." He'll feel better knowing he can talk without being put down or dismissed.

It's all right to let him follow a fad that's harmless and inexpensive. If you recall your own pre- and early adolescence, you'll remember longing to be like others. If a fad seems acceptable but you don't want to pay for it, let your child know he'll have to spend his own money.

When you have some negative feelings about a fad, explain your point of view and then, when appropriate, compromise. "You can listen to that music, but only with your door closed or with your headphones on." If you feel a fad isn't right for your child, set firm limits. "You can't wear pants with rips and holes in them." "You may not style your hair that way." (See pps. 179–183, "We Constantly Argue About Movies, Music, Video Games, and TV.")

While an interest in fads is normal, your child shouldn't become too involved with them. If he cares excessively about clothes and possessions, encourage him to broaden his interests. If he follows fads in an attempt to attract friends, help him find other ways to connect with peers. Finally, model the kind of common-sense approach to fads that you want your child to follow. If you communicate your sense of values, your child shouldn't get overly caught up in a quest for whatever is new.

My Daughter
Thinks She's Fat

Children learn at an early age to be aware of their weight. They see thin celebrities on TV and in the movies, and they look at ads for weight loss programs. They hear their gymnastics or wrestling coach urge them to slim down. They hear their parents talk about dieting or say "Don't eat too much or you'll get fat," and it becomes clear that thinness matters.

Many girls describe themselves as overweight. "I look so fat in this outfit." "There's so much flab on my legs!" "I hate the way I look!" Often a child with a good self-image says such things to receive a compliment or be reassured. "What are you worried about? You're so skinny." "I wish I were as thin as you are. You look great!"

Sometimes a child truly believes she's overweight even though she isn't. Parents have to evaluate their child's statements about weight, especially once she reaches 12 or 13. Some children these ages become so obsessed with "being fat" that their self-image suffers and they risk developing an eating disorder.

While it's natural for your child to pay attention to her changing body, try to keep her from dwelling on weight and appearance. Also keep her from dramatically altering her diet. Talking will help. "You seem to believe you're overweight and I'm trying to figure out why. Do your friends feel the same way about themselves?" Discuss physical development and body shapes as well as healthy eating, but don't lecture or your child will stop listening.

Focus on your child's interests and strengths. She may be less concerned about her body if her time is spent on enjoyable or challenging activities. Encourage her to pursue hobbies or sports. Help her get involved in volunteer work, art classes, rearranging her room, caring for a pet, or learning a new skill.

Examine your own eating habits and attempts to lose weight. If there's too much emphasis on dieting at home, your child may be influenced in a negative way. Be less open when discussing your weight, put out fewer magazines with dieting articles, and show your child, by your example, how to eat and exercise in a healthy way.

Your child may be concentrating on weight as a way of dealing with stress. She might find it easier to worry about being fat than to think about other problems. Try to find out if something is bothering her. Does she do well in school? Does she get enough attention at home?

Does she get along reasonably well with her siblings? Does she have conflicts with friends? Can she occupy herself when she's alone? If you can help eliminate some pressures in her life, her self-image will improve. This, in turn, should lessen her preoccupation with weight.

Make it clear that you love your child as she is and offer reassurance if she seems to need it. She may feel comforted to hear, "No, you're not fat." However, it's possible your words of praise and love will have little effect. If your child genuinely believes she's overweight, she'll continue to see herself that way.

If your child is 10 or 11 and talks about being too heavy, keep a watchful eye on her. If she's older, take her repeated complaints or changes in eating habits seriously. It's better to deal with the issue now, because the older she gets, the harder it may be to help her accept herself. If you are really worried, you might want to talk to a counselor. A professional can often prevent serious eating problems and help your child view herself more realistically.

My Child Has a
Weight Problem

Parents who believe their child is overweight may feel a mix of emotions. They might be disappointed and embarrassed because he doesn't fit some "ideal" or because his situation reminds them of their own struggles with weight. They may be worried about his health and self-image and feel very protective, especially if he's teased or ignored by his peers. Concerned parents may not know how to talk to their child or help him lose weight. And frustrated parents may sometimes explode in anger, belittling or blaming their child for something that may be beyond his control.

There are various reasons some children become overweight. Heredity and metabolism are contributing factors for most children. Some children have only a temporary weight problem that a growth spurt will eliminate. Some, who are not involved in activities outside the home, may spend too much of their time eating. Also, when a child is sedentary, he tends to gain weight.

If a child's emotional needs are not met, he may try to satisfy himself by eating. And naturally, eating habits have an effect: A child can gain weight if he has too many foods high in fat and calories, including such favorites as potato chips, hamburgers, pizza, ice cream, and candy. In rare cases, an underlying medical condition may cause a child to be overweight.

If you think your child has a weight problem, check with your pediatrician. You may find your child's weight is actually within normal bounds; if it's not, the doctor can explain why. She also can help plan a safe weight-loss program for your child, offer advice on talking to him about the issue, and refer you to a nutritionist.

Before discussing weight with your child, see if there are changes you can make that might help him. Alter your cooking methods (less frying, more grilling) and your buying habits (fewer chips, more pretzels). Encourage your child to be active; rearrange your schedule so you can drive him to practices, watch his games, take him to friends' houses, and generally make it easier for him to spend time outdoors.

It's important to plan what you want to say before talking to your child about being overweight. Ten- to 13-year-olds are very sensitive. Use a respectful tone and begin by speaking in general terms about appearances. "Lots of kids your age are concerned about how they look. How do you feel about your appearance?"

Your child may welcome a chance to talk. Find out

how other children have been treating him. Ask if he would like to try losing weight. If he says yes, work together on a plan to change his—and perhaps the whole family's—eating and exercise habits. The more cooperative your child is, the easier it will be to deal with his problem.

You may find, however, that your child becomes defensive when you bring up his weight. He may act distant or angry or speak negatively about himself. This is especially true if you are rigid or harsh or dwell on his appearance. He may overeat as a way of rebelling.

If you encourage your child to diet, he may resist your efforts, partly out of fear of drastic change. "Forget it! I just won't eat as much. I can plan my own diet. Let's not talk about it anymore!" Instead of arguing back, ask him for suggestions. An idea of his ("I just won't drink soda and eat dessert") may work. Offer encouragement. "You've got some good plans." "We'll try it your way first." "It may be hard, but I think we can do it."

Losing weight is very difficult, as most adults have learned, and your child may or may not be successful. Even if he loses weight now, he may regain it later. Be patient and supportive. Your child's self-esteem depends on your unconditional love and acceptance, not your evaluation of his appearance.

INDEPENDENCE

Does My Pre-teen Need Much Supervision?

Pre- and early adolescents often behave responsibly, showing that they understand safety rules and know right from wrong. However, they can also act irresponsibly, and for that reason they need consistent parental supervision.

When children are away from home, they're almost always supervised. They're watched at school, at camp, in organized sports, at social gatherings, and on field trips. Only at home are children these ages left without an adult for significant periods. And when children are unsupervised, especially if they're with friends, they take more risks and are likelier to end up in trouble.

In a spontaneous moment children forget rules, per-haps because of peer pressure or the desire for excitement. One 13-year-old walked to a pizza parlor at night, although she was told to stay indoors when her parents weren't home. An 11-year-old teased a 5-year-old neighbor until she cried. Two unsupervised 12-year-olds poured squeezable cheese on each other "for fun." A 10-year-old and her friends made a mess in the basement, leaving spilled soda, chips, and candy. Physical fights broke out at an unchaperoned party for 13-year-olds.

Although your child is becoming more independent, she needs your supervision. Your degree of watchfulness depends on her age and the circumstances. A 10-year-old obviously needs closer supervision than a 12-year-old. But whatever your child's age, you should know what she's doing and where she is, and you should set limits and offer guidelines. Your responsibility remains the same whether you're at home, working, socializing, or vacationing.

If your child has any kind of party, even one involving just a few friends, be home. If she's going to a party elsewhere, make certain parents will be present. Supervise sleepovers. Tell the children when they're making too much noise or staying up too late. If you're keeping an eye on things, you can end a troublesome situation or suggest alternative activities for your child, whether she's with friends or alone. "Why don't you play out front?" "I'll take you to the tennis courts." "Come get a snack." "How about reading the book you picked up at the library?"

As part of supervision, give frequent reminders about safety and manners. It's important that your child clearly understands your rules. She may still forget, bend, or break some, but as long as you're supervising her, she's more likely to act responsibly.

"Why Can't I
Go by Myself?"

Most parents had more freedom as 10- to 13-year-olds than they allow their own child. They roamed their neighborhoods, used public transportation, met friends at shopping centers, and walked alone at night. Their parents did not have the same worries about crime that contemporary parents do. The media constantly expose families to frightening stories of rape, abuse, kidnapping, and murder. Even schools have become places to fear as more children are found carrying weapons and acting in extremely aggressive ways.

Parents have mixed feelings about allowing their child independence. They want him to do things on his own, yet they're afraid for him. Children's feelings are more straightforward. Most don't share adult concerns; they think their parents are overly protective. "No one's going to hurt me." "I can take care of myself." "Nothing will happen. Why do you treat me like a baby?"

Since contemporary life has many uncertainties, it makes sense to err on the side of caution. Ten- and 11-year-olds naturally need to be watched more closely than 12- and 13-year-olds. But all children in this age group are vulnerable and need supervision and restrictions.

In general, insist that your child be with someone when he's away from home. Children are more vulnerable and likelier to get into trouble when they're alone. If your child is playing out of your sight, be sure he's with a friend or older sibling. "You can't go to the park by yourself, but I'll let you go with Brett." If you drop your child at a movie, make it clear you expect him to stay with his companions. "If you have to use the bathroom, go together."

When your child is with friends, check on him periodically or have him check in by phone or in person. If you allow him and a friend to separate from you at a shopping center, meet them at regular intervals. And if you let your child walk alone to a friend's house several blocks away, have him call you when he arrives and before he leaves.

Your child may be upset with the limits you impose, especially if you don't allow him to go places because he would be alone or because a location seems unsafe for someone his age. When your child asks "Why can't I go by myself?" you don't need to describe your fears. Instead say, "I'm not comfortable letting you go there. It would be fine if you were with someone or if you were older, but not now."

Your child may not like hearing this, but he won't be surprised. He's heard enough news and observed you long enough to know your concerns. He sees you lock your house and car doors. He's heard you voice your concerns. "Someone broke into a place near here." "I'm worried about my daughter's safety now that she's going off to college." "I don't like parking garages." "I hate to carry cash around." The world can be a frightening place. You don't want to scare or restrict your child unnecessarily, but you do want to supervise him enough—and limit his independence enough—to be sure he's safe.

Can My 12-Year-Old Babysit?

Babysitting is an excellent activity for early adolescents who are mature enough to care for young children. Babysitters learn to be responsible, creative caregivers; in return for their efforts, they earn money and feel the reward of doing a good job. With parental support, children as young as 12 can be successful sitters.

A 12-year-old generally does best with toddlers or older children. She may be overwhelmed by the tasks associated with a baby: changing diapers, warming a bottle, and dealing with crying. If a sitter is going to watch an infant, she should first spend time with the baby when his parents are home so she can practice caring for him.

Twelve-year-old sitters often want to work in pairs with a friend. Although they have to split their earnings, they like the security of having a companion. Unfortunately, sitters are sometimes less responsible when friends are with them and may need extra guidance and supervision.

Most babysitters are girls, but some boys also enjoy caring for young children. One boy said, "I'll babysit, but I won't change diapers." Most boys prefer sitting for youngsters who are old enough to play actively.

Before your child babysits, talk to her about how young children behave. She should know that they often act silly, enjoy attention, resist going to sleep, are fearful, have a hard time listening, cheat at board games, and can quickly get into trouble if left alone.

Give your child strategies for dealing with difficult behavior: She can try to distract a youngster, offer a snack, read a story, or pat the back of a child who can't sleep. To keep young children busy, she can draw with them, watch a video, listen to music, build, dance, or make up a story.

Safety is an important issue, both for your child and for the children she watches. To ensure your child's safety, check out any casual acquaintances or strangers who want to hire her. You can call them and chat, ask how they got your child's name, and set up a time when you and your child can meet them and their children. When you meet, try to evaluate their children's behavior—you may not want your child to sit for difficult youngsters. Tell the parents what time you want your child home and work out transportation arrangements. If you're uncomfortable, don't let your child take the job.

Talk to your child about keeping babies and young children safe. Since many parents don't give enough information to their sitters, you need to prepare your child. Discuss possible emergencies and tell her which questions to ask. She should find out how to get in touch with the parents and with you. She should also know what to do if someone knocks at the door or calls for the family.

Encourage your child to ask her employers practical questions too. How late does the child stay up? Can he play outside? Does he go to the bathroom alone? Will he climb out of his crib? What can he eat? What can your child eat when she babysits? Can she use the phone? Does she have to clean up?

As you may recall from your own days as a babysitter, any 12-year-old can be irresponsible at times. Even if your child is well prepared and mature, she may finish all the brownies, break something, or fail to pay enough attention to a youngster. Keep giving her tips, talking to her about each job, and stressing the importance of quality care. If you want to check on her while she works or simply reassure her, give her a call. She'll feel more secure knowing you're home and easily available.

Should My Child Stay Alone After School?

Many 10- to 13-year-olds spend considerable time on their own every day. While 12- and 13-year-olds may be mature enough to stay alone, 10- and 11-year olds are too young to be by themselves regularly or for long periods. Some local governments, through their social service agencies, set recommended limits on the amount of time children these ages can be left unsupervised.

Nevertheless, many parents feel they have no choice but to leave their young children alone. Parents must work, there are few sitters available, after-school care for this age group is hard to find, and alternatives are too expensive. Parents either convince themselves that their child will be all right or they go off to work each day feeling guilty and worried.

Few children, even 13-year-olds, would choose to

stay alone regularly. They'd rather be greeted after school and have the comfort of an adult or teenage sibling nearby. A child left on his own can become bored, lonely, or scared. He may hear strange noises or worry about frightening events he's seen on the news. Even his parents' warnings can be alarming. "Don't go outside." "Don't answer the door." "Never tell a caller I'm not home."

One child told her mother, "I hate being alone, but there's nothing I can do about it so I never complain." Many children don't speak up. They feel they have no control over the situation and they fear upsetting their parents. A child may sense that his parents don't want to know what he really thinks.

Many parents never ask their child what it's like to stay alone every day. They avoid discussion rather than risk hearing something that would make them feel guilty. When a child does voice opposition to staying by himself, his parents may say he's selfish or silly. "We do a lot for you. The least you can do is take care of yourself after school." Some parents rationalize. "It's a good time to get homework done." "You like to watch TV." "You can get your chores out of the way."

It's best not to leave your child home regularly, but if you have no choice, try to minimize his time alone. Arrange for him to go home with a friend. See if a neighbor can help out, if only to check on your child for a few minutes each day. Find out about afternoon activities at school and transportation home, such as a late school bus or a carpool. A classmate's parent may be willing to drive your child in exchange for a service you can provide, such as weekend babysitting. See if your child can stay after school to help his teacher, work in the library, or volunteer in the school office.

Consider letting your child invite a friend over as long as both children are mature and responsible, and the parents of the other child know you won't be home. However, if you have many doubts ("What if they do something unsafe?" "They might get silly or make a mess") wait until your child is older. Too often, children these ages do what they want, assuming their parents won't find out. "We can go to the park for a while." "Let's make some macaroni."

If you can't arrange supervision or companionship for your child, you can still provide home activities such as art projects, magazines and books, music to listen to, and puzzles. Leave a snack for him and a friendly note. Call shortly after you expect him home and give him time on the phone to tell you about his day in school. Let him know he can call you or a relative or friend if he wants to talk or if he has a problem. Keep a list of his friends' phone numbers with you so you can call their homes if you have to. You may be tempted to keep him busy with chores, but after a day of classwork, he may resent this. He needs a chance to relax.

Even if you can't change his circumstances, keep the lines of communication open. Listen to your child's thoughts about staying by himself and try to avoid lecturing. If you say "I have to go to work to pay for the things you need," he may stop sharing his feelings and instead feel guilty about being a burden. Let him express himself openly. Simply talking about being home alone may help both of you feel less stressed and more comfortable with the situation.

My Child Wants to Decorate Her Own Room

Children's bedrooms are the closest they have to "personal space." It makes sense that they want to individualize their rooms as much as possible. Yet many parents are reluctant to let their child do much, if any, customizing. "Your walls have to be white to match the rest of the upstairs." "Those posters are ugly—you can't hang them." "You can't have a beanbag chair. They collect dust."

Children with creative ideas become frustrated if they can't try them out. One boy wanted to hang his baseball hats on the wall. Another asked to string Christmas tree lights around her window. A 10-year-old wanted to put her mattress in a tent made of sheets.

If a child sees something appealing in a friend's room, she may want to copy it. "Shannon has a neat chair in her room. Can I get one?" "Alex's wall is covered with posters and it looks great."

A child who feels she has no control over many aspects of her life may fight to make decisions about her room. "Why can't I pick the color? Why do I have to have the pictures you like? It's my bedroom, not the living room!"

Although you may have firm opinions about how your house should look, at least consider some of your child's ideas. Whenever possible, allow her some flexibility. You may not want her to draw murals on her walls, as some children are allowed to do, but you can let her pick out pictures or make nonpermanent changes. If she wants to rearrange the furniture or put the mattress on the floor, let her try for a while and then switch back.

If your children share a bedroom, encourage them to compromise on temporary decorating changes, divide the space so each has room to individualize or take turns making changes.

If your child seems overly focused on redoing her room, think about her motivation. She may see decorating as an escape from other problems. If she's troubled, a new room arrangement won't help her feel better. However, if her social life, family life, and schoolwork are going reasonably well, you can assume her desire to redecorate is motivated by curiosity and creative ideas.

There are some real benefits to letting your child try her ideas. She may pick up some artistic or practical skills. She will feel more independent. And she may become more cooperative as she sees that you're willing to give her choices and some control.

Don't make your child promise to keep her newly arranged room neat. If she's already an orderly child, she'll automatically straighten up, whatever the arrangement. And if she isn't orderly, your insistence on being neat will only dampen her excitement. Instead of enjoying the new look, the two of you will end up arguing about her broken promise and your unrealistic expectations. It's better to treat cleaning up as a separate issue, not tied to your child's desire to personalize her own space.

Should My Child Decide How to Spend His Money?

Parents want their child to handle his own money responsibly. They want him to plan ahead, spend wisely, and save for the future. Most 10- to 13-year-olds, however, are less interested in being responsible than in buying what they want. This causes a dilemma for many parents. They know their child should make decisions and learn from his own mistakes, yet they want to keep him from wasting his money. These conflicting aims make it hard for parents to be consistent.

Sometimes the child's point makes sense. "It's my money. Why can't I get what I like?" "If I'm saving up for a video game, why do you care if it's expensive?" Parents points are also sound. "You shouldn't spend your money on junk food." "Get two sweaters instead of one expensive one." "Don't throw your allowance away on something that won't last."

In general, it's best to let your child decide how to spend his own money. But if you feel his spending is out of control, set limits. At a time when you're both feeling calm, talk about money. Listen to your child's side, even if he complains that you aren't being fair. You need to hear and understand him in order to know what will work. Tell him why you think saving and planning are important. Let him know you realize how difficult managing money can be and how easy it is to buy impulsively.

Together, come up with a management plan that allows your child flexibility. Within reasonable guidelines, you want him to make money decisions on his own. "You can spend some of your chore money as long as you also save some every week." "When I give you your allowance, I want you to put some aside to donate." If your child receives a significant sum as a gift for a birthday, Christmas, or a Bar Mitzvah, give him a portion to use as he wishes and have him put the rest in the bank.

To help your child make spending decisions, work out a budget. "How much money do you think you need for snacks and movies?" Offer specific compromises. "Instead of spending all your money now, buy the stationery this month and the shirt later." Encourage him to save by taking him to the bank to open or make deposits in his own account. He may be excited to see his money earning interest.

Don't be too restrictive or your child may feel resentful and start lying about money and purchases. But be firm about spending you don't approve of. "You can

get a different CD with your money, but not that one."
"You're too young to wear lipstick, even if you plan to
buy it with your own money." At these ages, your child
still needs clear limits.

Your child may want to use his money for an expensive purchase. One girl saved for a tennis racket; another planned to buy a tape player. A 13-year-old paid
for a lawn mower so he could earn more money cutting
grass. Be sure your child understands that spending
most or all of his money on a single item means he can't
make other purchases for awhile. Then, as long as the
item is one you would allow him to have, let him make
the decision. You might question his judgment, but he
will learn from the experience, whether he is ultimately
happy with his purchase or not.

Dealing with money is difficult, and you and your
child may continue to struggle with this issue. Keep
stressing your values, and show your child, by your actions as well as your words, how spending and saving
can be responsibly managed.

What Can My Child
Do over the Summer?

Children look forward to summer as a reprieve from school, a time to relax and have fun. Many 10- to 13-year-olds, tired of homework and busy schedules, want to hang around and "do nothing." At these ages, however, children still need supervision and planned activities during the summer, especially if both parents work outside the home.

Without a schedule of activities and an adult nearby, children may spend the summer watching TV, playing video games, eating junk food, and hanging out with other children whose parents aren't home. Leaving a child alone for a short time may be all right, depending on her age and maturity. But leaving a child alone or even in the company of a young teenage sibling every day for several months is a mistake. At best, the summer will be boring and aimless. At worst, the child will get into trouble.

There are many alternatives to staying home all day, some inexpensive or even free. Some children spend time at a pool, join swim teams, or play in various competitive leagues. Many park districts run supervised playground programs, and there are public and private day camps, specialty camps, sleepover camps, lessons, classes, and summer school programs. Many of these activities offer bus service or help parents arrange carpools.

If you aren't available to drive during the day, your child's choices will of course be determined by location, starting and ending times, and availability of transportation. As much as possible, try to enroll your child in programs of interest to her, or ones her friends will be attending. Children these ages are usually happiest doing whatever their peers do.

If your child is going to sleepover camp for the first time, the separation may be emotional for both of you. One mother said, "I'm a little nervous. Actually, I'm a lot nervous." To prepare your child, try to visit the camp ahead of time, look at pictures, or talk to someone who's been there. Talk to the camp director about concerns you or your child have. Let your child know that homesickness is natural, but that she'll get over it as she becomes involved in camp activities.

Some 10- to 13-year-olds want to work during the summer. Under supervision—yours, a neighbor's, or a friend's—your child can care for pets, weed, mow lawns, or babysit. You or a relative may also have odd jobs your child can do for pay.

Summer is a good time to catch up academically or pursue interests in learning and the arts. Encourage your child to read every day, keep a journal, write stories, draw, start a collection, make animated flip books, learn to type, use a computer, play an instrument, build, invent, make up plays, sing, act, sculpt, play chess, or learn a new craft. All of these activities can be entertaining, but too often they're associated with school or lessons. If you take a relaxed approach—and if you pursue such activities yourself—your child will find that learning on her own can be enjoyable and satisfying.

Finally, make time to be with your child, even if you work all day. On weekends, evenings, and days off, get involved in her activities and interests. Make plans together—go biking, camping, shopping, or swimming. Go to a museum, a baseball game, a historical site, the library, or a park. Get ice cream together or go on a picnic. Your child needs your attention, involvement, and watchfulness. She will be spending less and less time with the family as she gets older, so enjoy her company now, especially during the summer when schedules and people are most relaxed.

RESPONSIBILITY

Should My Child Need Reminders About Manners?

"**S**hake hands with Uncle Jack." "Remember to thank Mrs. McDonald for the ride." "Please hold the door." "Offer your friend a soda." Most parents don't understand why their 10- to 13-year-old still needs to be told these simple things. "I've been teaching my son manners since he was two years old and he still doesn't know how to act!"

The truth is, most children these ages continue to need reminders. It's hard for them to keep track of all the polite behavior they're responsible for—how to act in restaurants, how to greet guests, what to say to relatives, how to answer the phone, and how to treat friends and adults.

Children may also be unsure about politeness because they receive conflicting messages. Parents and teachers stress manners, but they sometimes demand good behavior in unpleasant ways. "I've told you a hundred times not to start eating till everyone's served. What's wrong with you?" A teacher admonished her students for interrupting: "I want you dumb kids to keep quiet." Children often imitate adults' behavior.

Most children display their worst manners at home, where they want to relax without worrying about politeness. Parents often despair when they imagine how their child acts with other people. But even the most forgetful children are better behaved when they're away from home. With company, they become more careful about manners and usually remember to at least say "please" and "thank you."

One 12-year-old demonstrated how she had folded her towel when she slept at a friend's house. Her mother was delighted because at home the girl usually dropped her towels on the floor. Another parent, who was often upset by her son's lack of table manners, was relieved when his dinner with relatives went well.

When you correct your child's manners, try not to be judgmental. It's better to say "Next time, please sound friendlier when you answer the phone" than "You're so rude on the phone!" Your child's forgetfulness is normal, and condemning him may only harm his self-esteem, since he still depends heavily on your good opinion.

If you anticipate a problem, prepare your child. Tell him ahead of time how you expect him to act when his grandparents visit, when he goes off in the carpool, when an important call comes, or when he sleeps at a friend's house.

The most important way to teach your child manners is to model polite behavior for him. If you treat him and others with respect, he will eventually take on your attitude as his own.

My Child Forgets
to Give Me Phone
Messages

A mother found a stray piece of paper with a week-old phone message: "Mom, call Carol." Two days after taking a message, an 11-year-old asked his father, "Did I tell you Uncle Mike called?" One woman's phone conversations often begin with her caller asking, "Did Jennie tell you I called?"

Many children forget to relay messages. Parents hope that their 10- to 13-year-old will be thoughtful and responsible enough to tell them about calls. But for a number of reasons, children often don't remember. A child who is distracted by TV or homework when the phone rings may not listen carefully. A child may become absorbed in an activity after taking the call and quickly forget the message. She may forget to write the message down immediately, which usually means she won't write it at all. Or, if the call doesn't pertain to her, she may soon stop thinking about it.

A child doesn't forget on purpose. She usually feels bad when she lets her parents down, and she doesn't intentionally disappoint or frustrate them. When confronted, however, she'll defend herself because she doesn't want them to be angry with her. "I was going to tell you later." "I started to write it down, but there wasn't any paper." "I thought I put her name somewhere." "I forgot. I can't help it. I'm not perfect."

Try to be patient—this behavior is very common. Keep telling your child how important message-taking is. Then, to make it easier for her and likelier that you'll get your messages, put pen and paper next to every phone. Create a central spot to leave messages. Tape a reminder note to the phone. Every time you come home, ask right away, "Any calls for me?" If you're expecting an important call, consider leaving your answering machine on so you'll be sure to get your message.

You may be tempted to teach your child a lesson by ignoring phone messages for her, but don't do this. When you say "See how it feels?" or "If you don't give me my messages, I won't give you yours," you teach your child to be spiteful. She'll be upset by your intentional act and feel that you've deceived her. Your tactic won't motivate her to remember messages. Instead it will show her that when she's disappointed in people's behavior, she can act without considering their feelings.

Focus on the times your child does remember to give

you a message. "Thanks for letting me know about Mr. Johnson's call. I'd been waiting to hear from him." And remember that most people who want to get in touch with you will call back—especially if they left their message with a child.

"Who Cares If
My Room's a Mess?"

"**Y**ou're not going out until you clean your room!" "I'm tired of telling you to straighten up." "Pick up your clothes and make your bed!" Most parents and children argue about messy rooms because parents care about keeping things neat and children don't. Most children don't mind waking up, going to sleep, playing, and doing homework amid a jumble of clothes, toys, books, and papers. They're unembarrassed for their friends to see a messy room, and they don't know why their parents get so upset.

A child may appreciate a clean room if someone else cleans it, but he won't straighten it himself because to him it's an unpleasant and unimportant task. "I hate putting clothes away." "All my friends have messy rooms." "Why make my bed if I'm going to sleep in it again?"

Parents have little success getting their child to think as an adult does about this issue, although they may be able to persuade or force their child to clean up, using a variety of strategies—paying him, bribing him, punishing him, or listing consequences. "If you don't keep your room clean, you can't have friends over." None of these techniques is particularly successful. A child may straighten up once or twice and then forget. Or he may clean his room in a halfhearted way, leaving much undone. Many children are punished over and over and still don't keep their rooms neat.

One of the most common parental threats—"If you don't clean your room, I won't do your laundry!"—often backfires. Parent and child stay mad, the room and laundry stay dirty, and the child picks up an I'll-get-back-at-you attitude from his parents.

Most children want to please, but they have trouble focusing on their rooms when their interests and energy are directed elsewhere. If parents continually attack their child for his messiness ("You're a slob!") he'll internalize their criticism. He'll feel upset and frustrated because he can't live up to their expectations.

The most successful and realistic way to handle cleaning up is to compromise, even though it means lowering your standards. If your child isn't keeping a neat room at this age, more punishment and harsh words won't help. Use a calm tone; if you're feeling tense after a frustrating day, wait a while before discussing cleanup.

Offer to help your child with his room. "I'll do this half of the floor while you work on the closet." Your child will appreciate your assistance, since straightening up alone can seem overwhelming. Suggest a timed cleanup. "See how much you can get done in fifteen minutes."

Don't worry about being consistent. Some days you'll care a lot about how your child's room looks and other days you'll shut his door and walk away. You might decide to ignore the mess unless company is expected. Or you might decide to wait until an every-other-week "family cleanup day."

Recognize that this is a common problem. You probably kept a messy room yourself when you were young. One mother, thinking her daughter was more disorganized than most children, was amazed to see the girls' bunkhouse at sleepover camp. Possessions were strewn everywhere and all the children seemed happily unaware of the chaos. "We just push the clothes to the bottom of the beds when we sleep."

The years from 10 to 13 are filled with turmoil, and you and your child may face some difficult issues. Try to put the problem of a messy room in perspective. As your child grows older, and as he eventually becomes an adult with his own home and possessions, he'll become much more conscientious about neatness and order.

How Can I Get
My Child to Do Chores?

Parents feel frustrated telling their child over and over to help around the house. They know that what they're asking—take out the trash, set the table, rake the leaves—is minimal compared to the full adult responsibility of running a household. They also know how much time they spend meeting their child's needs, driving her to special activities, shopping for her clothes, and preparing for her friends' visits.

Most parents believe that everyone in the family should routinely help out. They feel that doing chores will teach their child responsibility, help her mature, and let her make a contribution. But in reality, most children don't do regular chores without constant reminders, threats, bribes, and arguments. This was true when they were younger, it's true of 10- to 13-year-olds, and it usually remains true of children until they leave home. It doesn't seem to matter whether children are paid for their efforts or not. The problems involved in getting children to do routine chores often outweigh the benefits.

Children don't do their chores because the work is not a priority for them. They don't care about order and cleanliness the way their parents do. Dirty dishes, an overflowing trash can, toothpaste in the sink, roller skates left out, and baseball cards on the floor don't bother them. A child never complains to her parents, "The kitchen's a mess!"

Children often resent chores because their busy schedules leave little free time. A child who spends a full day in school, then goes to after-school care or a recreation class followed by an evening of homework, will not willingly wash the dishes. In addition, if stresses have built up during the day, chores can become a target of frustration. "Everybody always tells me what to do!" It's easier for a child to argue with her parents than with a teacher who may have been especially demanding earlier in the day.

When a child isn't interested in a routine chore, she avoids it. She'll procrastinate, move slowly, or be easily distracted. Many parents label this behavior laziness, but it is really a child's normal response to something she doesn't like.

If a child actually does do her chores, her parents may still be frustrated because of the quality of the work. The table won't really be cleared, crumbs will be left on the floor, the top will be off the toothpaste, and clothes will still be in a pile. When parents express their displeasure, their child becomes defensive. "Does it have to be perfect?"

If you want your child to do regular chores, you'll have to continually remind her. Try to stay calm. If you use a harsh tone, your child will be less cooperative: "I hate cleaning up!" You'll get a better response if you begin your reminders with "Before you leave, please . . ." or "Don't forget to . . ." or "I'd like your help with . . ."

Offer your child choices or vary her assignments. Some families have success with a job wheel of rotating responsibilities. Teach your child the most efficient way to do a task. She may resist an assignment because she's never learned how to do it. One boy told his mother, "I don't fold the laundry right because you never showed me how." Occasionally surprise your child by taking over one of her routine tasks. "I know you've been busy with schoolwork, so I'll vacuum for you this week."

If regular chores are causing too much conflict in your family, reconsider your expectations. A neat, well-managed home may not be worth the unhappiness and pressure your child feels. Many parents end up asking their child to do specific jobs as the need comes up, rather than assigning permanent tasks. "You take care of the basement while I straighten the living room." "Please clean your room before your friend gets here." "I want you to set the table tonight." "Give me a hand with these groceries." You will find your child more willing to help if the need is apparent and if she isn't overburdened by routine household tasks.

Of course, asking for help when you need it means the initiative is yours, not your child's. However, that is probably the case even if your child has regular tasks assigned, since she will need many reminders.

Everyone, including you and your child, grows up hearing adults stress the importance of cleaning up and doing household chores. Most people don't fully integrate and act on these messages until they are grown and on their own. The summer before freshman year at college, many parents are still trying to teach their child the best way to do laundry, mend clothes, and cook.

It's right to expect your child to help out. However, it's realistic to assume her help will be neither as frequent nor as efficient as you'd like. Try to be patient. And reinforce the good jobs she does, letting her know that you do appreciate her efforts.

Should the Dog Be My Child's Responsibility?

Taking care of the family dog is a big job, one many parents want their 10- to 13-year-old to handle alone. Parents hope that caring for the dog will teach their child to be responsible and to consistently meet another creature's needs. They also hope that the tasks involved—nurturing, feeding, cleaning, and exercising —will help their child mature and pick up valuable life skills.

In theory, that makes sense. But it's usually a parent who ends up walking the dog on wet nights, cleaning up after it on cold mornings, putting out food, and changing the water. No matter how hard parents push, most children aren't ready to take full responsibility for a dog.

Some of the tasks, such as buying food and visiting the vet, are usually impossible for a child to do alone.

126

Others, including all the walking and grooming, can seem overwhelming to children who have a lot to think about and keep track of. A child may promise to care for his dog, but he's only saying what his parents want to hear. He'd like to be helpful and he loves and cares about his pet, but the job is too big.

Knowing that it's typical for 10- to 13-year-olds to neglect some pet-care chores may help you be more understanding of your child. Although you may be disappointed, don't be too demanding. Harshness and threats won't make your child more responsible. Instead, he'll feel more stressed and angry and may take out his frustrations on others.

Offer to share responsibilities. Your child will appreciate your help if you don't make him feel guilty or neglectful. "Why don't I take over the morning walk for a while, since you're having trouble getting ready for school on time." Ask your child to do specific, short tasks. "Would you please feed the dog this morning?" Give frequent reminders. "Don't forget to feed Spike when you get home this afternoon." Praise your child when he does a good job, even if he helps only when you ask. "I'm glad you played with Missy. She really needed to run around."

While being responsible for a dog is a major job, your child may do well caring for a somewhat easier pet, such as a cat, fish, or a small caged pet like a gerbil or mouse. With only occasional reminders, he should be able to do all the feeding and cleanup. He may also succeed with a pet you want nothing to do with, such as a snake, spider, or lizard. Consider letting him have one of these as long as he understands the responsibility is completely his—no exceptions.

Although you may wish your child to care for your pet, particularly your dog, on his own, there are benefits to having the family take joint responsibility. Your child may not learn to be a solitary caregiver, but he will have the experience of chipping in and accomplishing something the whole family considers valuable.

I Want My Child
to Go to Bed and
Wake Up on Her Own

All parents want their 10- to 13-year-old to act responsibly at night and in the morning. They expect her to go to bed at a reasonable time so she can be healthy and alert, and so they can have time alone at the end of the evening. Parents also expect their child to get up and ready on her own each morning. But many children have trouble with daily routines. In some homes, bedtime and mornings are times for threats, frustration, and conflicts.

Children resist going to sleep because after a day of school, homework, and chores, they don't want their free time to end. They'd rather read, watch TV, talk on the phone, or play. Also, as children get older, they want more independence and may argue against a set bedtime. If parents are very rigid about evening routines, children may procrastinate as a way of rebelling.

And some children simply don't require as much sleep as their parents want them to have.

Morning conflicts can be as troublesome as bedtime ones, especially if everyone has to be out the door early. Some children, perhaps like their parents, don't function well when they first wake up. Others may be tired because they aren't getting enough sleep. If the family's morning is always rushed and stressful, a child may dawdle to avoid confrontations or to show resistance. She also may oversleep because she doesn't want to face problems at school, at home, or with peers.

If you and your child argue frequently about morning and evening routines, try changing your approach. Your child may be more responsible and cooperative if you're flexible and allow her some choice. As an experiment, push her bedtime back half an hour and see how she gets along, or try letting her stay up later than usual as long as she remains in her room, quietly entertaining herself.

You may decide to turn the decision about bedtime over to her. Many children who are given that freedom go to sleep at a reasonable time. When your child no longer has a rigid bedtime to resist, the evening routine will stop being an issue, and staying up late may stop being so attractive. She will probably go to bed when she's tired.

Letting your child choose when to go to sleep doesn't mean giving up all control. You can still set limits. "Ten o'clock is just too late for a weeknight." You can give reminders. "It's getting late. You should start getting ready for bed." If your child consistently stays up too long or is tired in the mornings, she's not ready to take responsibility for bedtime. Decide on an earlier time for her, but give her another chance to change in a few months.

Once your child feels she has some say in decisions about bedtime, she may be more willing to compromise in other areas of her life, including how she acts toward you and her siblings and how she reacts in the mornings. If mornings continue to be a problem even after you've eased up on bedtime, talk to her about it. "It seems to take you so long to get ready. What can we do to make things smoother?"

Your child may always wake up feeling grumpy. Try being patient and soft-spoken. A few minutes of understanding may ease her into the morning schedule. Rearrange the family's routine until you find an arrangement that works well; let your child shower last so she can have a few minutes more sleep, or have everyone get up ten minutes earlier so there's less hurry.

If nothing helps, try to find out why your child is reluctant to start her day. Is she having trouble at school? With peers? Is there too much tension at home? Are there too many rules and chores? Talk these issues over with her and let her know you're determined to help. You'll send a strong message of love and concern, which might motivate her to take more responsibility for her mornings and evenings.

My Child Is Getting Ready for His/Her Bar/Bat Mitzvah

Bar and bat mitzvahs are the traditional coming-of-age ceremonies for 13-year-old Jewish boys and girls. The ceremony is the culmination of years of general study plus an intensive six months of tutoring and preparation. The bar/bat mitzvah itself is a moving and spiritually fulfilling event. As the child reads and interprets his Torah portion, he offers wisdom and insight to his listeners. The periods before and after the bar/bat mitzvah are exciting, but they can sometimes be hectic or stressful.

As family members look forward to the ceremony, they may have ambivalent feelings. Twelve-year-olds wonder how they'll do. "What if I make a mistake?" "Will my speech be all right?" If children have a lot of schoolwork—especially if they've just begun middle school—the hours spent on Hebrew and bar/bat mitzvah preparation can cause considerable pressure. "I'll never be ready!" "All I do is homework and my Torah portion!"

Parents feel proud and sentimental as their child prepares to take on the responsibilities of a Jewish adult; however, preparations for the coming ceremony can put a strain on family life. Parents have to support their child as he learns and practices, and help him focus on the spiritual meaning of the event. They also have to take care of the practical arrangements, including scheduling lessons, driving, discussing the service, working with the rabbi and cantor, and reserving the sanctuary. If a party is planned, parents have to handle other details also: invitations, food, entertainment, decorations, and clothes. These responsibilities, added to everyday routines, leave many parents feeling stressed.

Siblings, too, can be affected by the bar/bat mitzvah. A younger child may be jealous. "It's not fair! I want my bat mitzvah when Jessie has hers." An older child who's already had a bar mitzvah may feel neglected as attention shifts to his sibling.

As you and your child approach the bar mitzvah, you can decrease stress by concentrating on the religious nature of the occasion, rather than on the preparations or the party. Talk about Judaism and your child's connection to past generations. Discuss Jewish history, holidays, and customs, the Holocaust, and the beliefs and history of other religions. Also emphasize the need to help others. Many families make community service and charitable donations an important part of the bar mitzvah period.

Get involved with your child's studies. Your interest, help, and support will make it easier for your child to learn his Torah portion and prayers and write his speech. Involve him in planning the service if the rabbi allows some flexibility. Your child may be able to choose prayers, recite a poem, or pick out appropriate music.

As you plan your party, let your choices reflect your family's style, budget, and values. You may have to resist pressure from relatives who want you to celebrate as they would, and you may have to resist internal pressure to "keep up" with friends and acquaintances.

Your child may be feeling pressures of his own. "I want kids to like my party." "Why can't we have the same things Aaron had?" If your child feels in competition with others, help him focus on the meaning of the occasion and on the honor of having friends and family with him. Whatever your celebration is like, your child, as the center of attention, will enjoy it.

It's appropriate to expect your other children to be happy for the bar mitzvah child; however, you may have to help them cope with jealousy. Encourage them to share their thoughts. "Brian's been getting a lot of attention because his bar mitzvah's coming up. What do you think of all this?" Spend extra time with your other children and involve them, if they wish, in some of the preparations.

Since bar mitzvahs are planned far in advance, there's always a chance of unexpected events, even disappointments. Illness, bad weather, or family conflicts may interfere with plans. A relative may not come. One of your child's classmates may have a bar/bat mitzvah on the same day as your child's. If you remain cheerful in the face of changes or disappointments, your child will follow your lead.

After the bar mitzvah, you'll feel happy and proud, but also somewhat let down after so much anticipation. Your child's feelings may be similar to yours, but he'll quickly be distracted by school, social life, sports, and other interests.

Your final responsibility is to have your child write thank-you notes. Make up a schedule. "I want you to write five cards every night." Give him a set of sample notes to follow. Sit with him and offer suggestions on personalizing his cards.

If your child received money as a gift, give him guidelines for handling it—have him save a large portion and keep a small amount at home to spend as he wishes. Some parents ask their child to give one of his presents to each of his siblings. Many parents ask their child to donate some gift money to charity. Being generous to those in need is a traditional Jewish value that is particularly appropriate at the time of a bar mitzvah.

PEERS

Peer Influence
Is Becoming Apparent

Parents worry about the effect of peer pressure on their child, especially once she turns 12. They hope she'll be strong enough to reject what she knows is wrong. But they understand from their own childhoods that resisting peer pressure is difficult. They also remember that children turn off the standard warnings and lectures: "If your friend jumped off a bridge, would you?"

Peer influence is an inevitable part of pre- and early adolescence. Children look to each other when choosing clothes, hairstyles, or music. They behave the way friends do because that makes them feel part of a group. Peer influence can often be positive. Children suggest good books, introduce friends to collecting and other hobbies, and encourage each other to study, take on neighborhood jobs, or be more polite. One 11-year-old told his friend, "You could be nicer when you ask your mom to do things for you."

Of course, there is also a negative side to peer influence. A susceptible child may be swayed to join a rough crowd or do something dangerous, thoughtless, or illegal: intimidate younger children, shoplift, get into fights, drink, smoke, or try drugs.

Children who are most vulnerable to peer pressure are those who don't receive firm, positive direction from their parents. A child may be largely ignored at home or forced to follow overly strict rules. As a result, she may look to friends for the attention and guidance she lacks at home. She may also be insecure. She follows her peers' bad suggestions to gain a sense of identity and feel accepted.

Most children these ages, however, aren't led into deep trouble by peers. A child chooses friends who are like her. And 10- to 13-year-olds usually can't be persuaded to violate their basic family values. They can be talked into occasional mischief, though, so parents have to stay alert. One 12-year-old snuck out of a school dance, violating the rules. He told his parents, "Scott and John told me to." He wasn't thinking about the worry he caused or the potential danger. He only considered the thrill of the moment and the fun of being with his friends.

Your child will be less vulnerable to negative peer pressure if she has a good self-image and a strong connection to her family. The more involved you are with her, the more she will want to please you. And if her identity is secure, she won't be so dependent on the approval of her friends.

Set limits on your child's behavior so she'll know what you expect and what the consequences will be if she disappoints you. If you find out after the fact that she did something you disapprove of, discipline her. (See pps. 157–160, "How Should I Discipline My Child?") Then start keeping a closer eye on her and her friends.

Discuss peer pressure with your child. Let her know you expect her to stand up to the group at times, even though you realize how difficult that can be. Try role-playing. "What would you do if a friend stole a necklace while you were shopping together?" "If everyone was teasing someone with a disability, how would you act?"

Share some of your own experiences. Let your child know that being independent won't mean the end of her social life. "Most of my friends decided to cut school lunch one day, but I didn't want to get into trouble. I felt really bad eating by myself. When my friends came back, they teased me about being scared, but we were still friends." Encourage your child to share her worries and talk about her relationships with peers. Although she's becoming more independent, your support and guidance are still essential if she's going to resist pressure to "go along."

"My Friends Get
to Do More Than I Do!"

When children complain "I never get to do anything good," parents sometimes react with anger and frustration. "So we're horrible parents." "Maybe you should go live with Ray if you think his parents treat him so much better." "Why don't you stop feeling sorry for yourself. You do a whole lot more than I did when I was a kid."

Children these ages want permission to do what their friends are doing, whether it's staying outside after dark, wearing makeup, seeing PG13- or R-rated movies, or going to an unchaperoned party. Children aren't thinking about safety, arrangements, costs, or their parents' values. And when they complain, they're not deliberately trying to hurt their parent's feelings or act in inconsiderate ways. They're simply focusing on their need to be part of the group.

When a child repeatedly makes requests that his parents consider unreasonable, they may feel frustrated not only with him but with his friends. Parents wonder if their child is too dependent on his peers, and they worry that particular friends may be bad influences. "I don't trust David's judgment. I don't want you playing inside his house."

Parents also become frustrated with other parents, especially those they believe are too lenient. One mother refused to let her 10-year-old walk around a mall with a classmate who was allowed to spend hours at the shopping center unsupervised. "I don't care if Emily's mother lets her go by herself. I'm not comfortable letting you wander in the mall without an adult."

If your child complains about the restrictions you impose, try to listen patiently without responding immediately. He may just need to vent his feelings: "It's not fair! I'm always the first one who has to go home." "You're too protective. You worry all the time." He may not argue with your decisions if he feels heard.

Avoid angry, defensive statements, even if you feel unfairly attacked. When your child says "You never let me do anything," calmly explain why you're refusing permission for a particular activity; if your refusal is nonnegotiable, let your child know that there's no point in trying to persuade you. "Every family is different. These are our family's rules."

Offer acceptable alternative activities. "Call Lee and ask if he can come over." "See if you can find a friend who'd like to go to the pool." "Let's stop at the video store and get something good to watch."

Periodically reevaluate your rules; you should gradually allow your child more freedom as he gets older. But as you ease some restrictions, continue to give your child firm directions. "Stay with your friends." "Check in with me." And continue to say no to anything that seems unsafe or inappropriate. Throughout these pre- and early adolescent years, your child needs clear limits, guidelines, and supervision.

Should I Limit
Phone Use?

As pre-teens become increasingly involved with friends, they spend more time on the phone. Some make short calls for practical reasons. "When's the game?" "Do you want to come over?" "What's the homework?" Others spend hours on the phone every day. They call each other to talk about school, tests, social activities, who likes whom, clothes, weather, sports, music, movies, and families. They even call to "watch" television together. "We've both got 'The Simpsons' on."

Parents wonder why their child wants to make and receive so many calls. Adults try to minimize their own time on the phone, especially in the evenings. Yet some children want to talk constantly, even to people they've just seen. A girl leaving a friend after a sleep-over may yell "Call me!" as she gets in the car. One parent described his 13-year-old's visits to her grand-parents: "Hi, Grandma and Grandpa. Can I use your phone?"

There are many reasons children like to call each other. Talking on the phone is an activity—some-thing enjoyable to do, especially during the long afternoons when parents aren't home. It's a good way to stay busy.

Phoning also gives pre-teens a chance to talk about their feelings. Ten- to 13-year-olds share less and less of their personal lives with their parents. They'd rather discuss family and social problems with friends, who won't criticize or lecture them. Peers are generally more sympathetic than parents are.

Another reason friends call each other is to finish conversations they've started in school. Although class-mates are together all day, they rarely have time to so-cialize other than during recess. Since talking too much in class or at lunch can get children in trouble, they call each other at home to talk in detail about the day's events.

Most parents don't want their child to spend a lot of time on the phone. They worry about the hours away from homework, chores, and physical activity. They dislike the frequent interruptions caused by phone calls and get angry when the line is busy. "I'm expecting an important business call" sometimes gets the response "But I have to tell Jen just one more thing." In addition, parents don't like siblings arguing about phone use. "You always let Michelle talk longer." "Jon's on the phone all the time. It's not fair!"

Some parents try to control phone calls with rigid rules, but this rarely works. Tracking calls and strictly allotting phone time takes considerable effort, and there are always special circumstances. If parents forbid all weeknight social calls, their child may end up sneaking calls or lying. "I wasn't on the phone." "I just had to ask a question about our math assignment."

One solution to arguments about phone calls is flexible scheduling. "You can use the phone from seven-thirty to eight and then it's Tim's turn." If you try this, make sure all family members know there will be exceptions to the schedule. An important call might come in, someone may have to return a call, or an extra few minutes may be needed to finish a conversation.

You can also try a flexible approach without specific scheduling. If you remind your children to be patient and considerate of each others' needs, they may be able to juggle phone time according to daily circumstances. You and your spouse should also follow whatever guidelines the family agrees on. Your child will feel angry and uncooperative if all of your calls, even unimportant ones, take precedence over hers.

If you find your child is not spending enough time on homework or other responsibilities, limit her use of the phone. "You can only make a call when your assignments are done." "You have a big project due in two days. No calls until it's finished." You should also limit your child's calls if you want to spend more time with her. "I just got home and I'd like to hear about your day. You can call Emily later."

If your child spends too much of her free time on the phone, suggest alternatives. You don't want phone use to be a substitute for other activities. Try interesting her in drawing, playing a game, using a computer if one is available, writing, reading, going outside, having a friend over, or taking part in after-school activities or sports.

When your child does use the phone, be sure she knows how to act responsibly—no late-night calls received or made, no trick calls, no calls with silent friends eavesdropping, no rudeness to adults who answer the phone. Since telephone technology changes constantly, be aware of the ways your child uses, or misuses, services such as conference calling.

Some new services may help alleviate your family's arguments about phone use. If you receive a lot of calls, consider a "call-waiting" option. Use an answering machine to eliminate the need for some calls and to allow you to screen others. If lack of privacy is an issue, try inexpensive extension phones or a cordless phone.

Some families add a second phone line, but such an option is costly and may not stop the conflict. Whatever phone services you try, continually encourage your children to share, to be reasonable, and to show respect for each other.

My Child Feels Unpopular

Being part of a group is very important to pre- and early adolescents. They spend a great deal of time thinking about their popularity and the main factors that affect it: personality, athletic skills, and looks. "Will Scott invite me to his party?" "Am I as pretty as Lisa?" "Is Ian a better basketball player?" "Who will I walk to school with?" "Will Samir like me if he knows I'm friends with Joey?"

Children constantly weigh their relative positions in a group. Since friendships frequently shift at these ages, a child may feel liked one week and rejected the next. Sometimes children who have been best friends through much of elementary school drift apart because of differing interests and developmental changes; if one joins a new group, the other may feel temporarily alone. A pair of friends may be broken up by a third child who bonds with only one of the original two.

Children who leave others out in these ways are usually not deliberately cruel. They simply don't think about the consequences of ending friendships. Instead they concentrate on their own interests and desires to be liked.

Parents have mixed reactions to their child's worries about popularity. At times they're impatient with concerns about trivial incidents. "I'm sure Beth still likes you. It doesn't matter if she says hi to Anne first."

However, parents suffer along when their child feels truly rejected. They're upset by his hurt feelings, tears, and confusion. Yet they can't make the situation better, as they could during earlier years, with a phone call to another parent or an invitation to a new friend. Parents can say "Call someone else from your class," but they can't force others to accept their child and they can't create friendships for him.

What they can and should do is listen and offer reassurance. A child who is vulnerable needs a great deal of support, and if he doesn't get it from his parents, he won't get it at all. Parents must remind their child that he is worthy of friendship and love and that he will get through these bad times.

When your child talks about feeling unpopular, be a sympathetic, understanding listener. If he expresses inevitable doubts about his place in the group, offer quick reassurance and help him put his experience in perspective. "Everybody has an occasional bad day when they

151

play baseball. I'm sure your friends didn't mean to insult you."

If he describes deeper hurt, offer comfort. "This is a hard time for you. But you're a great kid and it won't be long before you make new friends." Remind him of his strengths. "You're very funny and you have so many talents—you can sing, you're a wonderful student, you play soccer, you're a nice kid who makes other people feel good."

Pay enough attention to your child's friendships that you know when things aren't going well. If your child doesn't talk about social problems, raise the subject yourself. "I notice Nick doesn't call here anymore. Are you two still friends?" "It's hard to talk about feelings, but I'd like to help you."

Share stories about your own experiences while growing up. "I know how you feel about Josh. There was a really popular cheerleader named Sandy in my class. I was jealous of her and hated her and wanted to be friends with her at the same time." Let your child know that he will get over his social difficulties, just as you got over yours.

If you think your child is losing friends because of negative behavior, encourage him to be less aggressive and self-centered. "Try listening to other kids' suggestions more often." "Don't be so tough on your friends." If your child's shyness keeps him from joining a group, encourage him to invite friends over individually.

Talk to your child about why children exclude each other. He should understand that former friends probably didn't mean to hurt his feelings—they just developed new interests. Likewise, if your child has given up some of his own friendships, help him see what the consequences may have been.

Although popularity is a big issue at school, most teachers and administrators don't deal with it, especially in middle school. However, if your child is still in fifth or sixth grade, ask his teacher to help him get to know potential friends. She could seat your child with special classmates or have him work with them on group projects.

Throughout these years, encourage your child to reach out to new friends and spend time with children who like him. Support him and encourage his sense of self-confidence. As long as he has basic good feelings about himself, he'll get through the inevitable periods when he feels left out by his peers.

EVERYDAY CONFLICTS

How Should I
Discipline My Child?

All parents wish their pre- and early adolescent had more self-control and better judgment. Parents want to spend less time supervising and disciplining their child, yet children these ages continue to be irresponsible at times. They may make bad decisions, spend too much money, stay out too long, show disrespect, curse, skip a class, or neglect chores.

In some families, discipline becomes a major issue: Children misbehave frequently or in serious ways and parents struggle for control. In other families, misbehavior is minor and discipline is not a source of stress. The difference often lies in the nature of the parent-child relationship.

Parents who show continual love and respect for their child, spend time with her, and communicate their values give her a strong incentive to behave well. She values her relationship with them and wants to please, not disappoint them. In addition, the guilt she feels if she lets them down helps keep her from doing something wrong, even when her parents aren't there to supervise.

To improve your child's behavior, begin by strengthening your relationship with her. The closer you are, the more effectively you can shape her conscience and help her become self-disciplined. Take an interest in her activities and include her in yours. Let her know that you care about her opinions and feelings, and that your love—although not necessarily your approval—is unconditional.

If your child does something wrong, show your anger and disappointment, but don't yell insults or use put-downs and sarcasm. It can be useful to stir up some feelings of guilt or shame to help your child remember how to act. "When you didn't call, I was worried that something happened to you." You want your child to think about the consequences of her behavior. She may act more responsibly next time in order to avoid feeling bad. One 12-year-old said, "Feeling guilty is worse than getting grounded."

Talk to your child about her misbehavior. "Why did you go home with Jeremy when I told you not to?" Listen to her side, then explain what was wrong with her actions and what the consequences will be. A discussion is more effective than a lecture. Your child will tune you out or react angrily if you do all the talking and she's forced to listen to long, negative comments about herself.

Don't slap or hit your child. Her behavior will become worse rather than better. She'll be so angry that she'll continue to misbehave or she'll aim her resentment at siblings and peers, becoming aggressive and selfish.

Although physical punishment is not effective, let your child know her misbehavior will have consequences. Use whatever seems to work best: grounding, taking away allowance or privileges, refusing permission to use the phone or TV.

Be sure the consequences you pick will have the desired effect—to get your child thinking about and improving her behavior. If you always ground her for a day or two, she may continue to misbehave, knowing the punishment is short-lived and not severe.

On the other hand, don't be too harsh or strict. If your child is grounded for weeks or months or constantly loses her allowance, she'll focus on her unfair treatment. She'll be unwilling to change her behavior, and if she's forced to, she'll misbehave in other ways. She may become sneaky, resentful, or withdrawn.

In general, be flexible about consequences. If one technique doesn't work, try another. You may need to talk more and punish less. Or, if you depend too heavily on reasoning with your child, you may need to set firmer limits with heavier consequences. If you're having trouble finding an effective punishment, ask your child what she thinks a fair consequence for her misbehavior would be. While her suggestions may be too mild or too harsh, you may get some useful ideas.

Remember that setting limits alone won't solve ongoing behavior problems. Continually work on establishing better communication and understanding. Look for the causes of inappropriate behavior. Are there frequent family conflicts? School difficulties? Does your child feel neglected or less favored than a sibling? You may need a therapist's help to find the roots of discipline problems.

Finally, set a good example. Show your child, through your actions, how you expect her to behave. Be thoughtful, concerned, and courteous with others as well as with her.

I Want to Be
More Patient

Parents' impatience with children takes several forms. One is situational—parents lose their tempers and snap at their child for his misbehavior. A second form is more general. Parents lack the patience to listen to their child, play with him, accompany him to activities, watch him play sports, or help him with schoolwork. Both kinds of impatience can have a negative impact on children and make parents feel guilty.

All parents lose their patience at times, especially when they're rushed or busy or feeling badgered by their children's demands. "I'm trying to pay bills. Don't make so much noise." "I can't drive you to Glen's again." Parents experiencing stress at work or at home are especially likely to snap at their child.

Such impatience due to circumstances is often mild and temporary. More harmful to children is constant criticism and rudeness. Parents with a low tolerance for frustration may routinely yell at their children, ridicule them, and call them names. "Don't be so stupid! I've told you a hundred times not to leave the front door open." "All you do is whine." "I'm not a servant. Make your own lunch."

Parents with high expectations and a strong desire to be in control can become intolerant when things don't go their way. They expect perfection. If their child can't meet their standards, they react with harsh impatience. In the process, they may hurt their child's self-confidence, harm family relationships, and cause their child to become less, rather than more, cooperative as he copies the treatment he's received.

In less dramatic ways, parents also show impatience when they neglect to make time for their child. It takes a reordering of priorities to put aside adult concerns and answer a child's question, look at his model rocket, walk him to the basketball court, go to his school assembly, or read a book to him. Even the busiest parents can stop what they're doing for a few minutes several times a day to concentrate on their child. But some parents—even ones with time to spare—often don't put their child's needs first.

Becoming a more patient parent takes effort and may require a change in attitude, priorities, or behavior. If you are easily frustrated, try to make your life less stressful by easing up on your expectations. It's more important to spend time with your child than to have a clean house. It's better to stay calm during the early evening than to prepare a complex dish for dinner. If work or family problems are difficult to cope with, you may find stress-reduction techniques useful. You can learn about them from books, magazines, or classes.

Use a respectful tone of voice when you talk to your child—the same tone you'd like him to use. Instead of shouting "Hurry up!" or "Get going!" say "Please hurry or we'll be late." The more you take your child's feelings into consideration, the better his behavior is likely to be. In the long run, he'll respond more positively to your calm tone than to rude orders.

Make a decision to spend more time with your child. Put your book or work down periodically, stay off the phone at night, forgo some evening plans, and calmly get involved with your child. This is not always easy, since it means giving of yourself without necessarily receiving an immediate return. But there are definite benefits. Your child will have you as a model of tolerant, patient behavior. He'll feel better about himself because you're interested in him. And the relationship between the two of you will improve, making it easier for you to react to his behavior in a mature and patient way.

I Want My Child to Be More Honest

"It wasn't me who left food in the basement." "There wasn't any change from the money you gave me for the movies." "You never told me I was supposed to feed the cat."

Children lie for many reasons. The main one is to avoid getting into trouble. A child who fears punishment may lie, hoping she'll avoid the consequences of misbehaving. The harsher the possible punishment and the stricter and more inflexible her parents are, the more likely the child is to bend the truth.

Children also lie to get out of chores or schoolwork ("Can I stay home today? I have a really bad stomachache") or to feel part of a group. "Yeah, I saw that video too." Children may use lies to impress others and prop up a poor self-image. "I got an A on that test." "I go to Florida all the time." "The coach said I was the best on the team."

Some children lie because they're able to get away with it. Their parents fail to set adequate limits and don't teach the value of honesty.

To get your child to become more honest, be unambiguous about your expectations. "I won't accept lying." "People in a family have to trust each other. If I can't trust you, I can't let you do the things you ask and I can't count on you to be responsible." "I always expect you to tell me the truth."

Be a good role model. Since your child will know when you're lying to her, be honest about everyday events as well as important issues such as illness, separation, and unemployment. Show your distaste for acquaintances, public figures, and publications that exaggerate or distort the truth.

Make a clear distinction between acceptable white lies told outside the family and the need for honesty within the family. Your child can understand that white lies are sometimes necessary for safety or to keep from hurting someone's feelings. "I had to tell her I liked her hair. She just had it cut." "If someone calls when I'm not home, say I'm in the shower."

Set firm limits and let your child know there will be serious consequences if she doesn't tell you the truth. Punishment can include grounding, added chores, or loss of allowance or privileges. There's no need to yell or speak harshly. Instead use a firm, calm tone to discuss the seriousness of lying.

You may find that punishment isn't needed at all. If you emphasize your disappointment and hurt, your child may decide that the consequences of lying—including feeling ashamed and guilty—are worse than the consequences of confessing to the original misbehavior. Appealing to your child's conscience this way will work best if you have a good relationship with her and if she values your approval. An important way to get your child to become more honest is to strengthen the ties between you.

When your child does tell the truth about misbehaving, praise her honesty. If she lies, but later offers a genuine apology for doing so, accept the apology. You will still have to decide if the original misbehavior requires punishment. Being honest shouldn't wipe out the consequence of negative actions, but you may decide to be a little more lenient to encourage your child's honesty.

Don't manipulate your child into telling the truth ("I won't punish you. I just want to know where you were this afternoon.") and then come down harshly ("You know I don't want you at the mall. You're grounded for a month!"). Your child will only have more incentive to be dishonest next time.

If your child regularly lies and exaggerates, try to find out why. Are you too lenient? Too inflexible? Does your child feel jealous of a sibling? Do you spend enough time with her? Do you give her enough positive feedback and encouragement? Is family discord causing stress? If lying is a symptom of deeper problems, limits and punishment won't improve your child's behavior. You'll need to change the circumstances that keep her from being truthful.

My Child Is
a Bad Sport

All parents want their child to be a good winner and loser. They want him to try his best in every situation and accept any outcome with grace. Parents have a strong stake in their child's sense of sportsmanship. They believe his behavior reflects on them, and if he's a poor sport, they're not only disappointed and angry, but embarrassed.

Children like to win games, have the highest grades, get the starring roles, be first in line, win elections, and get prizes. Most of the time, though, a child is not number one. Defeat and mistakes are inevitable. Occasionally a coach or teacher will give a good sportsmanship award or credit a child with trying. But there are few rewards for those who lose, and some children have a hard time accepting that.

A child who is a poor sport loses control easily. He

may be moody or angry. He may have outbursts and throw a tennis racket, tear up a paper with a poor grade, kick a chair, or curse at an opponent. He may also be disrespectful to a teacher, counselor, umpire, coach, or parent as he vents his frustration. On a team he may belittle his peers. "Why can't you hit the ball?" "What kind of throw was that?" "It's your fault we're losing the game."

Sometimes a child will get down on himself and question his abilities. "I'm never entering another stupid art show again." "I always lose the camper contests. I must be the worst kid here." "I'll never get on a select soccer team."

While no one likes to lose, there are several reasons why some children become poor sports. A child may have unreasonable expectations and become upset when he fails to live up to them. His parents may encourage his high standards by overemphasizing winning. "I hope you beat this kid because I hate the way he plays and I can't stand his father."

Parents may be impossible to please. "You're not trying hard enough." "I know you could win the spelling bee if you just studied more." "Too bad you came in second." Some parents don't set firm enough limits on their child's displays of bad sportsmanship. They encourage his misbehavior by not trying to stop it.

Poor sportsmanship is sometimes a sign of low self-esteem. A child who lacks confidence may get easily upset when he doesn't do well. Lack of sportsmanship may also indicate that a child is in over his head, frustrated because he's competing in situations where he doesn't stand a fair chance. A child who doesn't enjoy competition may not react well, no matter how much support he receives.

Most poor sports are aware of being out of control and would like to change their behavior. However, they don't know how to handle difficult situations. They need help and guidance when they make a mistake or lose a competition.

Tell your child how important good sportsmanship is. Talk about how other people—friends, acquaintances, famous competitors—react to success and adversity. "She lost the election for mayor, but she still promised to support her opponent." "When that tennis player threw his racket and cursed, everybody booed." Let your child know that it's also important to be a good winner, one who is gracious rather than cocky.

Before your child enters a competition, remind him about his behavior. "You look better when you show control." "Have fun." "I don't want to hear you yell or complain." Set limits on his negative actions and discuss consequences. "If you keep throwing your helmet, I won't let you play." Praise signs of good sportsmanship. If he handles himself well, reward him with a hug, a pack of baseball cards, a note, or an ice-cream cone.

Evaluate the competitions your child participates in. Perhaps they're too stressful for him. Some children are spurred on by competition, while others are upset by too much of it. Your child's sportsmanship may improve in a less intense atmosphere.

If you suspect that your child's attitude is rooted in a poor self-image, think of ways to increase his confidence. Spend more time with him, have fun together, encourage him in all his activities.

Try to be a good sport yourself. Do you react angrily when things don't go your way at work, at home, on the road, or during leisure time? Do you put too much pressure on your child? Do you give positive feedback only when he wins? If you change your attitude, you may see a difference in your child's behavior.

Talk to coaches or teachers about helping your child become a better sport. Suggest they hold a team or class meeting on the values and characteristics of good sportsmanship.

At times your child may have a legitimate reason for feeling "things aren't fair—I shouldn't have lost." An umpire may make a bad call. A teacher may make a mistake. Another player may cheat. One girl became upset in gym class as the teacher continually called on boys to demonstrate volleyball techniques. When the child asked why, the teacher said, "I don't want the girls to be embarrassed if they miss the ball." Your child may have a right to complain, but he should learn how to handle situations appropriately, without acting like a bad sport.

I Wish My Child
Were More Self-
Confident

One of the most important tasks parents have is to consistently let their child know she is capable, loved, and worthy of attention. A child's self-esteem is based largely on feedback from her parents. If they show they value her, she will generally feel good about herself. If they concentrate on her faults, she may develop a poor self-image.

It's normal for 10- to 13-year-olds to have changing opinions and fleeting self-doubts. One moment they boast about their skills and the next moment put themselves down. "I'm a good baseball player." "I can't sing." "I'm too tall." "I'm smart and do really well in school." "I can make people laugh." "I stink at lacrosse." "I'm so fat and ugly." "I do everything wrong."

Because children's feelings about themselves fluctuate, it's important for parents to emphasize strengths rather than weaknesses. The attitude a child develops about herself during preadolescence, whether positive or negative, helps determine the direction she'll go in when she enters adolescence, a period of even greater uncertainty.

Some parents are not supportive. In an effort to improve their child or to express frustration and disappointment, they speak harshly. "You're such a slob." "Why can't you behave like your sister?" "What's wrong with you? Why don't you speak up?" "You run too slow." "You'll never get to college at this rate." A child who hears these messages feels she can never please her parents or live up to their standards. Her grades, her appearance, her abilities, or her personality will never be good enough. In such circumstances, it's hard for her to develop confidence.

Some parents who speak negatively were themselves criticized as children and may have grown up with a lack of confidence. Even though they once struggled against harsh words and treatment, they repeat the pattern with their own children.

Other adults, particularly teachers, can influence a child's self-image. Schools rarely work at building confidence or offering praise. More often, students are reprimanded for turning in work late, making mistakes, or talking. One child may get a poor grade on a project even though she put in hours of hard work. Another child who is forgetful may be embarrassed in front of the class. "You're one of the laziest kids I've ever taught."

Coaches too can affect a child's sense of confidence. An encouraging coach can make a child feel good, regardless of her athletic ability. A demanding coach can make even a skilled young athlete doubt herself. "One more bad pitch and you're out." "What's wrong with you? Go after the ball."

You probably know if your child lacks confidence, since a poor self-image is hard to hide. Your child may frequently put herself down or say "I can't" or "I'm no good at . . ." or "I'm the worst on the team." If you see a consistent pattern of negative thinking, you need to help your child feel better about herself.

Start by evaluating the messages you give her. Do you encourage her self-doubt? Are your expectations too high? Do you respect her feelings? Are you too demanding? Do you tell her you love her? Are you hard to please? Do you dwell on her weaknesses but take her strengths for granted?

Give your child more verbal rewards. Praise her accomplishments and point out her talents and endearing traits. Talk often about her successes and ignore or minimize her faults. Encourage her and offer support when she takes risks such as trying out for a school play.

Talk, as a family, about what you like in yourselves and each other, and what you have to offer others. "Your smile makes other people feel happy." "Why do you think Betsy and Megan like you so much?" Discuss issues that contribute to your child's lack of confidence. "Would being taller really make you a better person?" "What's wrong with being shy?"

Help your child find activities in which she can succeed. If she's not good at team sports, have her try an individual sport such as swimming, tennis, karate, or gymnastics. Encourage her to pursue special interests in computers, music, art, or dance. Involve her in community service: She'll feel needed and she'll feel good about helping others.

If your child is discouraged about her schoolwork, talk to her teacher. Help your child with difficult lessons and assignments; consider hiring a tutor, if needed, and investigate special programs that might make your child feel better about her ability as a student. (See pps. 189–192, "My Child Complains About School.")

Once you start talking to your child and treating her in a more positive way, you should see changes in her behavior and attitudes. She may seem more confident and smile more. She may also treat friends and family members in nicer ways as she begins to feel better about herself. In all areas of her life, improved self-esteem will help your child feel happier, more satisfied, and more successful.

My Child Is
a Show-off

"**H**ey, watch me!" "Look what I've got!" "I'm buying a better one!" "See what I can do!"

All children show off at times. They demonstrate their skills or show possessions they're proud of. Bragging can be a way to get peer approval or to feel equal to others. Sometimes it's done in fun. As long as a child is generally caring and responsible, occasional showing off is not a problem.

Some parents actually encourage their child to be a show-off. A parent who repeatedly says "You're the only skilled one on the team" or "You're much prettier than the other girls around here" will reinforce self-centered ways. A child who is not taught to consider others' feelings won't realize that most adults and children find showing off offensive.

While some children are encouraged in their negative

behavior, most who constantly boast and act silly do so because they are insecure or unhappy. A child who behaves this way may feel unpopular with his peers or unloved by his parents. He may show off in order to hide disturbing feelings.

Such a child often creates problems. At school he may be the "class clown," and at home he may argue frequently with his siblings. With friends, he may be silly and disruptive. Such acting out is a way for the child to release frustration and seek attention.

If your child consistently shows off, try to find out why. You can begin by asking him what he thinks, but you may find him confused and unable to explain his feelings. Ask yourself these questions: Do I give my child enough positive attention? Do I spend enough time with him? Do I encourage him and compliment him? Does he feel overshadowed by his siblings? Is he jealous of them? Does he have friends? Does he do well in school? Is he compensating for what he sees as a defect, such as being overweight or small for his age?

Also ask yourself if you are somehow encouraging your child to show off. Do you talk about respecting other people? Do you make it clear that bragging is unacceptable?

As you begin to understand your child's behavior, you can plan ways to change it. If you haven't been setting firm enough limits, let your child know what your expectations are. Talk to him about the importance of being considerate, modest, and patient.

If you have been setting limits on showing off, becoming stricter will not change your child's behavior.

He will only feel angry, pressured, and upset at not being able to please you. He may continue to show off and become louder and more boisterous to rebel and express his frustration.

Instead, help him solve the problems that cause him to show off. If he's doing poorly in school, work with him on lessons and assignments and talk to his teacher. If he has few friends, make it easier for him to join a team or have classmates over. If he's overweight, ask your doctor for advice and encourage your child to become more active.

If the problem is your child's relationship with the family, work on changing the way you treat him and his siblings. Concentrate on his strong points rather than his weak ones. Don't compare him to his siblings. Try to give him enough positive attention so that he feels good about himself. The more confident he becomes, the less showing off he will do.

We Constantly Argue About Movies, Music, Video Games, and TV

"**Y**our radio is too loud!" "That movie is way too violent for you." "Turn the TV off!"

As children get older, they increasingly struggle with their parents over control of leisure activities. Children want to relax with the TV, as adults do, satisfy their curiosity by watching R-rated movies, listen to popular music, and play video games until they win. To a child, these are enjoyable activities. They allow her to do what her friends do, stay busy, and avoid stressful situations. A child doesn't think about the value of these pursuits or the messages she's receiving. She just wants to pass the time and have fun. "Why are you so critical, Mom? It's only a movie!"

Parents do think about consequences. They know that time spent in front of the TV is time taken away from schoolwork, physical activity, socializing, reading, and creative hobbies. And they worry that exposure through the media to violence, sex, profanity, alcohol, drugs, and questionable morality may have a harmful effect on their child.

The main issue for parents is deciding what to let their child see and do, and for how long. Parents must set limits, but they also have to compromise, allowing their child enough freedom so that she won't pursue forbidden activities behind their backs.

If you have rules about TV watching, make exceptions for special programs, nights when homework is done early, rainy days, and other circumstances. Allow her to spend more time on a video game when a friend is over or when the game is new. If she's begging to watch a rented video that you consider marginal, watch it with her and then talk about it. And let her play her music loudly at times when no one will be greatly disturbed.

Provide attractive alternative activities for your child. Enroll her in classes; encourage involvement in sports; have books, art materials, puzzles, and games available. Suggest she read the paper. (She can find movie, record, TV, and concert reviews there.) Spend time doing things as a family. Plan trips to museums, stores, or parks and have your child bring a friend along.

Follow your instincts. You know what's appropriate for your child and approximately how much time she needs for homework, physical activity, socializing, and relaxing. Decide what you're comfortable allowing her to do, and decide on your "absolute no's." Then don't be swayed by what other children are permitted to do. Families rarely have identical values.

If you and your child argue about movies, try to read as much as you can about the ones she's interested in. Talk to people who've seen them. If a movie seems acceptable, let your child go. But if you believe it will frighten her too much, be too intense, or expose her to sights and ideas you disapprove of, keep her home. Don't rigidly follow the ratings: "You can't see an R movie until you're thirteen." Some R-rated movies may be acceptable if you don't mind your child hearing profanity, while some PG movies may glorify immoral acts and characters.

Choose home videos as you would theater features. If a movie's not right for your child, don't let her see it. Restrict access to cable movies, using the mechanical control feature on the cable box if necessary, and let your child know what kinds of movies she should and shouldn't watch when she's at friends' homes.

Handle TV viewing in a similar way. Let your child watch programs that are good or at least harmless. Preview an episode of a questionable series or read about made-for-TV movies ahead of time to see if they're acceptable. Keep a copy of a TV schedule at work so you and your child can talk by phone about afternoon shows. Monitor how much time she spends watching. TV should be a minor entertainment, not a major occupation that takes up a disproportionate amount of time. Your child should save TV watching for the short breaks between the truly important activities in her life.

Video games, by their nature, require a lot of playing time. It's all right to let your child occasionally spend hours at a time at a video game, as long as she doesn't do it regularly and as long as she's devoting enough time to schoolwork, socializing, and outdoor activity. Since you may not approve of some games, question your child or read reviews before making a purchase. One mother told her son, "You can get a game, but not one that shows any torture or realistic killing."

Finally, like many parents, you may argue with your child about her choice of music. Try to be patient. Occasionally listen with her and let her turn the car radio to her favorite station. She'll appreciate your interest, and you'll learn about her taste. In general, let her listen to the music she likes, but keep her from buying tapes or CDs you strongly object to. Educate yourself by looking for reviews and questioning other children and adult listeners. It's hard to control what your child hears, especially on the radio, but you can express your displeasure with certain lyrics and ideas.

You don't have to worry about lyrics having a negative influence on your child as long as your relationship with her is strong and she's doing well in school and with peers. If she's having trouble at home and elsewhere, she may be more susceptible to the negative messages in her favorite songs. Rather than censor the music, try to make positive changes in your child's life. Strict limits alone may only encourage her to lie about what she's doing.

When you set limits on any of your child's leisure activities, be calm and don't make fun of her choices.

You want to criticize a program or product, not your child. Instead of shouting "Only a stupid person would waste time on such trash," say "Don't you think this program makes girls and women seem unintelligent? I don't like our family watching shows with that message." Your child might be more willing to follow your suggestions and rules if you explain your objections and treat her with respect.

How Should I
Handle Profanity?

All 10- to 13-year-olds use profanity at times. They may curse, as adults do, out of frustration, anger, or sudden pain. They may also use profanity when they're with friends, as a way to feel part of the group or to act older. It's easy for children to learn profanity—they hear it on TV, in movies, and from peers and parents.

Most adults don't like to hear children swear. They may tolerate their own child's occasional outburst but otherwise feel that cursing at these ages is rude and disrespectful. Many parents set firm limits. "You're not allowed to use that language here." "I don't talk that way and I don't want you to." "Don't ever use those words around adults."

Children who are generally secure and know their parents' expectations are not likely to use excessive profanity. One child said she wouldn't curse a lot, even if her parents said she could. "I know you don't like it." Some 10- to 13-year-olds ask permission before using profanity. "I have to tell you what this kid said in school. Can I say the 'b' word?" After a losing soccer game, a frustrated player asked, "Is it all right to cuss now?"

Parents can usually limit profanity at home, but they have less control when their child is with peers. Experimenting is common, and a child wants to be like his friends. If they use profanity, he will also.

One 11-year-old told his mother, "Kids cuss all the time at camp. Everyone does it when they aren't around their parents." After school vacation, another child said, "I'll be back with my friends, so I'll probably start cursing again." It's common for children to tell each other silly or dirty jokes and to use profanity, especially with friends of the same sex. However, most children these ages know it's unacceptable to speak the same way in front of adults.

Some children, though, don't get clear messages about cursing. Their parents might use a lot of profanity themselves or may not communicate values. Children who don't learn limits at home are likely to be reprimanded by other adults, including teachers, coaches, and their friends' parents: "Please watch your language!"

If you generally feel good about your child's behavior, try to accept occasional profanity. Continue to set limits and discuss standards of behavior. Remind your child that cursing is not appropriate social behavior.

If your child uses more profanity than you would

like, consider modifying your own language. If you frequently curse, your child may be following your example. Also, limit his exposure to movies and TV shows that contain bad language.

If you feel that your child uses excessive profanity, ask yourself if underlying problems are causing him anger and stress. Your child may be cursing in order to express his frustration. If he's having trouble with schoolwork, peers, family members, or self-esteem, setting limits on profanity will not improve his situation. You'll have to identify and begin to resolve your child's basic problems in order to see an improvement in his language.

BIGGER
PROBLEMS

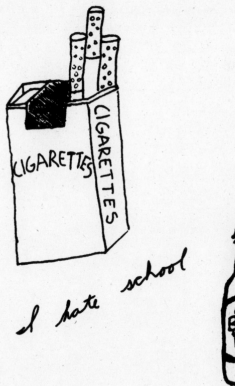

I hate school

My Child Complains About School

Many children don't like school. They complain about the work, the rules, the teachers, the bus ride, their classmates, or homework. Sometimes the problem centers on the child. Her unhappiness may be a symptom of stress at home, low self-esteem, or problems with peers. At times a child may "hate" school because she isn't doing well. The work may be too hard. The class may be too large or the setting too distracting for her to concentrate. A child starting middle school may need time to adjust.

Often, however, the problem is school itself. Children have valid complaints. "Coloring is a waste of time." "Field trips are no fun because you spend your time taking notes and doing what the teacher says to do." "The book reports we turn in are stupid. You don't even have to read the book." "I worked so hard on this paper and she marked it all up and said to do it again. Next time I'm only writing a little."

Schools have a responsibility to teach subject matter, help students become independent and responsible learners, and encourage them to think critically and analytically. Children should be respected and teachers should be tolerant of mistakes. Schools should also help parents understand how the education system works and what they can do to help their child. Unfortunately, many schools fail at these tasks.

Classroom rules and teaching methods often bore children and discourage learning. "I don't like science because we never do experiments." "We have to do the same work as everyone else, even if we already know it." "You're never allowed to talk." "She always calls on the same kids." There is rarely enough flexibility, spontaneity, or creativity in schools.

"Gifted and talented" classes are often especially disappointing. In many schools, the accelerated and regular curriculums are the same. A gifted child is simply expected to do more of what everyone else is doing— four similar worksheets, for example, instead of two. One mother took her child out of his middle school gifted program. "The only extra thing the G-T classes had was more busy work!"

Since children don't have the power to change what happens in the classroom, they complain, hoping adults will help. Some parents listen sympathetically. Like their child, they're frustrated. They want her to be an active, involved learner, but they fear she won't be motivated by daily, uninspired lessons.

Other parents don't want to hear complaints. "I got through the system and so can you." These parents may defend the status quo and blame their child for not going along with teachers' demands. "If Mrs. Cooper won't give you extra credit, she must have a good reason."

If your child is unhappy in school, she needs your help. Try to find out what's wrong. If family problems are interfering with schoolwork, make an effort to relieve your child's stress. If work seems too hard, talk to the teacher, find a peer who can coach your child, hire a tutor, or do tutoring yourself. If your child has continuing difficulty with schoolwork or with a particular teacher, ask if your child can switch to another class. If you're financially able, consider a private school that addresses your child's needs.

Get involved in your child's education. Encourage her efforts, help with homework, talk about what she's learning, and be supportive, even when she gets a low grade. Provide the stimulation that may be lacking in school; this will increase your child's interest and skills. Go to museums, special exhibits, libraries, bookstores, nature centers, and the zoo. Talk about articles from newspapers and magazines. Do research together. Stop in educational stores to pick up interesting materials. And make reading—individually or aloud—a priority.

Talk to your child about her dissatisfaction with school. She may be very perceptive about the problem or she may have only a vague idea of what's wrong. Many 10- to 13-year-olds lack the experience and understanding to analyze their situation. But most can offer some ideas for improvement. "Why can't we work in groups?" "Why can't we make suggestions about subjects to study?" "I wish the teacher would stop putting kids down." "If she were nicer, I'd ask more questions."

To help change your child's school situation, become an active member of the PTA and get to know the teachers and principal. Talk to them about your child's problems, offer your suggestions, and ask for theirs. If you're calm and respectful, they should be willing to listen. Contrary to parents' fears, most teachers won't react negatively to a child whose parents have a complaint. If you're not happy with your local school's response, take your issues to the school district administration. However, be realistic about the improvements you can bring about. School systems change slowly, if at all. Rather than wait, do all you can to keep your child interested in learning.

What If My Child Experiments with Alcohol? Drugs?

Parents want to believe that their 10- to 13-year-old won't try drugs or alcohol. After all, pre-teens and early adolescents are constantly exposed to anti-drug messages ("Just Say No!") in school, at home, and in the media. Children hear about celebrities' drug addictions and overdoses, about drunk-driving fatalities, alcoholism, and drug- and alcohol-related violence. Parents hope all this information, plus the values stressed at home, will keep their child from trouble.

However, children are curious, and drugs and alcohol are easily available, even to elementary school students. The same media that broadcast the "bad news" about drugs also glamorize drug and alcohol use. Many teen heroes are drug users, and many rock songs, videos, movies, and TV shows make drugs and alcohol seem acceptable and even desirable.

Children, especially seventh- and eighth-graders, can usually point out the "drug group" at school. One 13-year-old frequently tells his parents about kids who buy drugs at his suburban school. "They stand at their lockers and pass little bags to each other." Children are fascinated by the subject of peers' drug use. They want to know who does it, why, and how it feels.

Many children want to experiment. The most vulnerable ones, the ones who actually try drugs, are those who are usually unsupervised, who feel consistently left out socially, who have too much stress in their lives, or whose parents abuse alcohol or drugs. If such children don't experiment at these ages, they are likely to in high school, where exposure, access, and peer pressure are greater.

Peer pressure plays a big part in early drug use. Children are easily influenced by their friends and fear rejection for not "going along." A child needs a strong counterinfluence at home, giving him the reasons and the inner resources to resist.

The best way to help your child is to let him know that drug use and underage alcohol use is absolutely wrong. Give a clear, strong message that will become part of his conscience. He'll need to remember your words and values when friends urge him to experiment. Don't waffle, even if you think that a little drink or occasional marijuana is not so bad. It is bad, especially at these young ages. What starts out as fun can quickly lead to a pattern of abuse and permanent damage.

If you suspect that your child is already experimenting, act quickly. Ask him about drug use, keep a watchful eye on his behavior and friends, and search his room and belongings. If he is drinking or using drugs, don't try to deal with the problem entirely on your own. Get advice right away from books or a counselor experienced in treating adolescent drug use. (See pps. 203–204, "Suggestions for Further Reading.")

While you're getting help, try to learn why your child turned to drugs. Is he escaping from his problems? Who are his friends? How does he spend his free time? Are you home enough? Is school too stressful? What family values do you stress? Do you try to hide substance abuse by adult family members?

Stopping drug use early is important, but it takes strength and perseverance. You'll not only have to work on the immediate problem, but establish an involved and positive relationship with your child so he can move in a better direction with your love and support.

I Think My Child Smokes Cigarettes

Parents become quite upset if they suspect their child has been smoking. Children constantly hear that smoking is unhealthy; when they were younger, they probably urged their parents to quit. "I'll never smoke! It's ugly and bad for you!" "People who smoke cigarettes are stupid!"

But some children change their minds when they hit pre- and early adolescence. Peer pressure, curiosity, and the media can make smoking seem attractive. Children who smoke at these ages are often just experimenting. They force themselves to inhale, then cough, feel nauseous, and stop. That's usually the end of it.

However, some 10- to 13-year-olds habitually smoke. They may be children with difficult home lives and little interest in school or sports. Or they may be smart, active students from stable homes. Young smokers don't necessarily fit one stereotype.

Sometimes a child will talk at home about classmates who smoke. "Just don't tell their parents." A child who speaks often about smokers may be testing her parents' reaction. She doesn't realize that while her parents may be only mildly interested in another youngster's smoking, they would be furious if their own child started.

Aside from a desire to experiment, children these ages smoke because they think it makes them seem "cooler" and older. Slick advertising campaigns further this myth. A child may know all about the health risks associated with tobacco, but she'll smoke anyway because she doesn't believe bad things will happen to her.

Pre-teens are focused on the here and now. They think "I can always quit later" or "Teenagers don't get lung cancer." The more support a young smoker has from her peers, the less likely she is to think about future problems.

If you find out your child has experimented with tobacco, express your disapproval, talk about the harmful effects, and then—if she's stopped smoking—let the matter drop, although you should continue to keep a watchful eye on her.

However, if you suspect that your child is a regular smoker, treat her habit as a serious problem. Verify her smoking by searching her room for cigarettes and matches. Most children don't hide things very well. Confront her. "I smell smoke when you come in the house." "Kathy's mother told me you were smoking at the mall." "I found a cigarette lighter in your jacket pocket." If she lies, don't accept what she says, even though you might prefer to avoid the issue.

Let her know how you feel. "I'm very angry and disappointed." "You made a bad choice and I won't accept it." "Smoking at your age is terrible." Tell her about the major risks of smoking, but also talk about the other problems it causes, such as stained teeth, an unpleasant odor, and lack of wind for sports. These immediate effects might impress her more than long-range threats to her health.

If you feel partly responsible for your child's smoking, change some of your behavior. Give up smoking. Spend more time with your child and supervise her more closely. If you believe that she is continuing to smoke, keep raising the issue and giving a consistent message. Monitor her activities and friendships, and consider telling her friends' parents about the problem. Be persistent—your child's health is at stake.

Does My Child
Need Therapy?

Because 10- to 13-year-olds change so rapidly, it can be hard for parents to distinguish between emotional problems and the normal upheavals of pre- and early adolescence. Is a child depressed or just moody? Seriously unmotivated or merely preoccupied? Deeply angry or beginning the inevitable separation from the family?

Parents won't necessarily find answers to such questions in discussions with their child. Children these ages sometimes avoid sharing their thoughts with adults whom they see as sources of criticism, lectures, and unwanted advice. Parents may be left to evaluate their child's situation based on their own observations.

Identifying serious, persistent problems is usually not difficult. Most parents know to seek help if their child shows clear signs of drug or alcohol abuse; an eating

disorder; serious depression; criminal behavior, including the threatening use of weapons; or suicidal behavior.

Beyond such clear-cut cases, many parents are confused. They don't know if their child needs help ("It's
just a phase. Everybody gets depressed sometimes.")
and they don't know if they "believe" in counseling for
any but the most critical problems. Some parents as-
sociate therapy with shame and embarrassment. They
fear the implication that something is wrong with their
child; they worry that a counselor will blame them for
their child's problems. They may also worry that their
child will speak badly of them or reveal family secrets.
Such fears keep many families from getting the help
they need.

If you are unsure about your child's situation, ask
yourself these questions: Has the troubling behavior
been going on for a long time, despite your attempts to
help? Do teachers, coaches, or other parents complain
about your child? Is your child frequently angry? Does
he regularly put himself down and act discouraged?
Does he do poorly in school? Does he have trouble
making friends? Is he consistently jealous of his siblings? If your child has continuing difficulties in several
areas of his life, he may benefit from professional help.

He may also benefit if his problem is an unreasonable
fear or phobia. A counselor experienced in treating pho-
bias can desensitize your child. One boy who greatly
feared elevators was able to ride them alone after six
counseling sessions. A child who feared airplanes flew

off on vacation with her family after only a few weeks of counseling.

You might turn to therapy to help your child deal with recent or continuing trauma, such as the death of an immediate family member or close friend, divorce, or a frustrating stepparenting situation. During counseling, your child can express his pent-up anger, fear, and doubt to a sympathetic, nonjudgmental listener.

If you decide to try therapy, ask your pediatrician, family doctor, or local medical bureau for referrals. Set up an appointment with the therapist for a consultation without your child present. Describe your concerns and ask for advice. You may hear that therapy is not necessary and you may get helpful suggestions for improving your situation at home.

If the therapist does recommend counseling, talk to your child about it. Explain what therapist do. "There are some problems we can't solve on our own." Let your child know there is nothing wrong with seeking therapy. In fact, some of the celebrities he admires may be quite open about seeing a therapist. Tell your child about the benefits of therapy. "Dr. Graham will help you feel happier and better about yourself." "Susan is used to talking to children about their fears." If your child resists, don't give up on counseling. Ask the therapist for the best approach.

Therapy can take a number of forms: individual, group, or family counseling. Any one, or a combination, can be effective. If your child is seen individually, schedule occasional consultations with the therapist so you can learn more about your child's situation. You may also want to join a parents' discussion or support group in which your questions and concerns can be addressed.

Therapy in any form can be prohibitively expensive. Most health insurance companies and HMOs cover a percentage of the cost. Local and state government agencies as well as some nonprofit organizations offer therapy at reduced or sliding scale fees. In addition, many private therapists are willing to lower their fees when patients are unable to pay the full rate.

Although it can be difficult to start therapy, it's wise to work on emotional problems while your child is 10- to 13-years-old. As he gets older, his situation and behavior will only become more complex. If you get help for him now, your family will have a much easier time as he moves through adolescence.

SUGGESTIONS FOR FURTHER READING

Cline, Foster, M.D., and Jim Fay. *Parenting Teens with Love & Logic: Preparing Adolescents for Responsible Adulthood.* Colorado Springs, CO: Pinon Press, 1992.

Elkind, David. *All Grown Up & No Place to Go: Teenagers in Crisis.* Reading, MA: Addison-Wesley, 1984.

———. *The Hurried Child: Growing Up Too Fast Too Soon.* Reading, MA: Addison-Wesley, 1988.

Faber, Adele, and Elaine Mazlish. *How to Talk So Kids Will Listen and Listen So Kids Will Talk.* New York: Avon Books, 1982.

Gardner-Loulan, JoAnn, Bonnie Lopez, and Marcia Quackenbush. *Period.* Volcano, CA: Volcano Press, 1991.

Ginott, Dr. Haim G. *Between Parent & Teenager.* New York: Avon Books, 1971.

Krueger, Caryl Waller. *Single with Children.* Nashville, TN: Abingdon Press, 1993.

LeShan, Eda. *When Parents Separate or Divorce: What's Going to Happen to Me?* New York: Macmillan, 1986.

Madaras, Lynda, with Dane Saavedra. *The What's Happening to My Body? Book for Boys*. New York: Newmarket Press, 1991.

———. *The What's Happening to My Body? Book for Girls*. New York: Newmarket Press, 1987.

Maxwell, Ruth. *Kids, Alcohol, & Drugs*. New York: Ballantine Books, 1991.

McGinnis, James, editor. *Helping Teens Care*. Crossroad, NY: Institute for Peace and Justice, 1991.

Mooney, Belinda Terro. *Leave Me Alone: Helping Your Troubled Teenager*. Blue Ridge Summit, PA: TAB Books, 1992.

Steinberg, Laurence, Ph.D., and Ann Levine. *You & Your Adolescent: A Parent's Guide For Ages 10–20*. New York: Harper & Row, 1991.

Strasburger, Victor, M.D. *Getting Your Kids to Say "No" in the '90's When You Said "Yes" in the '60's: Survival Notes for Baby Boom Parents*. New York: Simon & Schuster, 1993.

Weinhaus, Evonne, and Karen Friedman. *Stop Struggling with Your Teen*. New York: Penguin, 1988.

Westheimer, Dr. Ruth. *Dr. Ruth Talks to Kids: Where You Came From, How Your Body Changes, and What Sex Is All About*. New York: Macmillan, 1993.

Wexler, David B. *The Adolescent Self: Strategies for Self-Management, Self-Soothing, and Self-Esteem in Adolescents*. New York: W.W. Norton, 1991.

FOR THE BEST IN PAPERBACKS, LOOK FOR THE

In every corner of the world, on every subject under the sun, Penguin represents quality and variety—the very best in publishing today.

For complete information about books available from Penguin—including Pelicans, Puffins, Peregrines, and Penguin Classics—and how to order them, write to us at the appropriate address below. Please note that for copyright reasons the selection of books varies from country to country.

In the United Kingdom: For a complete list of books available from Penguin in the U.K., please write to *Dept E.P., Penguin Books Ltd, Harmondsworth, Middlesex, UB7 0DA.*

In the United States: For a complete list of books available from Penguin in the U.S., please write to *Consumer Sales, Penguin USA, P.O. Box 999—Dept. 17109, Bergenfield, New Jersey 07621-0120.* VISA and MasterCard holders call 1-800-253-6476 to order all Penguin titles.

In Canada: For a complete list of books available from Penguin in Canada, please write to *Penguin Books Canada Ltd, 10 Alcorn Avenue, Suite 300, Toronto, Ontario, Canada M4V 3B2.*

In Australia: For a complete list of books available from Penguin in Australia, please write to the *Marketing Department, Penguin Books Ltd, P.O. Box 257, Ringwood, Victoria 3134.*

In New Zealand: For a complete list of books available from Penguin in New Zealand, please write to the *Marketing Department, Penguin Books (NZ) Ltd, Private Bag, Takapuna, Auckland 9.*

In India: For a complete list of books available from Penguin, please write to *Penguin Overseas Ltd, 706 Eros Apartments, 56 Nehru Place, New Delhi, 110019.*

In Holland: For a complete list of books available from Penguin in Holland, please write to *Penguin Books Nederland B.V., Postbus 195, NL-1380AD Weesp, Netherlands.*

In Germany: For a complete list of books available from Penguin, please write to *Penguin Books Ltd, Friedrichstrasse 10-12, D-6000 Frankfurt Main 1, Federal Republic of Germany.*

In Spain: For a complete list of books available from Penguin in Spain, please write to *Longman, Penguin España, Calle San Nicolas 15, E-28013 Madrid, Spain.*

In Japan: For a complete list of books available from Penguin in Japan, please write to *Longman Penguin Japan Co Ltd, Yamaguchi Building, 2-12-9 Kanda Jimbocho, Chiyoda-Ku, Tokyo 101, Japan.*

FOR THE BEST IN CHILD CARE BOOKS, LOOK FOR THE

☐ **EYEOPENERS!**
How to Choose and Use Children's Books About Real People, Places, and Things
Beverly Kobrin

Open your child's eyes to a whole new world! Information and excitement awaits your child between the covers of nonfiction books. Beverly Kobrin, a gifted teacher, shows you how to find—and make the most of—the best children's non-fiction books available.   *0-14-046830-7*

☐ **LOVING YOUR CHILD IS NOT ENOUGH**
Nancy Samalin with Martha Moraghan Jablow

Filled with practical solutions to everyday problems and compassionate advice on communicating with your child, *Loving Your Child Is Not Enough* will help you avoid confrontation and truly enjoy your child's growing years.
0-14-009473-3

☐ **THE NEW READ-ALOUD HANDBOOK**
Revised Edition
Jim Trelease

Raise a reader! If you have children or know children who can't read, won't read, or hate to read, this classic, common sense-based book will help you awaken the book-lover inside them.   *ISBN: 0-14-046881-1*

☐ **FIRST FEELINGS**
Stanley Greenspan, M.D. and Nancy Thorndike Greenspan

With *First Feelings* you can help your child develop confidence and security that will last a lifetime. It is the first book to show parents how to understand—and be prepared for—a baby's emotional changes.   *0-14-011988-4*

You can find all these books at your local bookstore, or use this handy coupon for ordering:

Penguin Books By Mail
Dept. BA Box 999
Bergenfield, NJ 07621-0999

Please send me the above title(s). I am enclosing _____
(please add sales tax if appropriate and $1.50 to cover postage and handling). Send check or money order—no CODs. Please allow four weeks for shipping. We cannot ship to post office boxes or addresses outside the USA. *Prices subject to change without notice.*

Ms./Mrs./Mr. _____

Address _____

City/State _____ Zip _____

FOR THE BEST IN CHILD CARE BOOKS, LOOK FOR THE

☐ **UNPLUGGING THE PLUG-IN DRUG**
Marie Winn

The first complete guide to holding your own "No TV Week," *Unplugging the Plug-in Drug* explains TV addiction and how to fight it. You'll learn how to make a week without TV a time for more reading, more play, and a more enjoyable family life. *0-14-008895-4*